Three Awakenings

A Spiritual Memoir

by

Theresa Crater

Satiama
PUBLISHING

https://satiamapublishing.com/

First Printing, 2022
ISBN (Print) 978-1-7373757-8-4
ISBN (E-book) 978-1-7373757-9-1
Library of Congress Control Number 9781737375784
Written by Theresa Crater
Book Cover Design by Amy Koenig
10 9 8 7 6 5 4 3 2 1

BISAC CODES:
OCC031000   **BODY, MIND & SPIRIT** / Ancient Mysteries & Controversial Knowledge
OCC016000   **BODY, MIND & SPIRIT** / Occultism
OCC000000   **BODY, MIND & SPIRIT** / General

Satiama, LLC
PO Box 1397
Palmer Lake, CO 80133
(719) 487-0424
www.satiamapublishing.com
PRINTED IN CHINA

Dedicated to All Seekers

Contents

Endorsements

"A fresh, intimate peek into the experience of spiritual illumination. A soul-satiating account."

~ Jodine Turner, Author of *The Awakening: Rebirth of Atlantis, The Keys to Remember, Carry on the Flame: Destiny's Call, Carry on the Flame: Ultimate Magic,* and *The Hidden Abbey*

"From her beginnings in the 'enlightened' 1970s TM movement...to her discovery of a Crystal Skull named "Max" (who speaks to her and subsequently 'introduces' her to her Egyptologist husband) to their later excursions to Egypt, where she communes with the Sphinx and Sekhmet...this memoir is filled with 'You just can't make this up' moments! I closed *Three Awakenings* feeling more knowledgeable...AND excited about the spiritual possibilities that await me. I couldn't put this book down!"

~ Caryl Englehorn, Owner of Angel Speak Intuitive Channeling and Medium

"Crafting a boldly honest and compelling spiritual memoir, Theresa takes readers on an intimate journey of discovery of self and path. We have the pleasure of sharing her powerful, deeply transformative experiences. I especially enjoyed the potent and fascinating journeys that occur between her moments of awakening. Ultimately, Theresa reminds us of the importance of deep connection to ourselves and the ineffable. Delightfully insightful and intriguing. This is a book that will appeal to everyone whether you are a new seeker or the someone who knows the path well. "

~ Ellis Nelson, Author of *Into the Land of Snows, Timeless Tulips, Dark Diamonds- A Ghost Story, Elephants Never Forgotten*

"This is a delightful story of one woman's experiences with Unity Consciousness, sprinkled with pearls of wisdom plucked from the oyster bed of her journey. Insightful and thoughtful, I enjoyed it very much."

~ Maighread MacKay, *The Lake Scugog Mysteries and Finding Charli*

Forward

I KNEW OF THERESA CRATER LONG BEFORE we actually met. I was aware that she was a prolific writer and that we shared an interest in spiritually powerful places. She wrote novels set in Egypt and Glastonbury with a metaphysical twist. I also knew that she was half of a power couple; her husband Stephen Mehler was a well-known expert in all things Egypt and author of excellent books on the subject. I related to Theresa and Stephen perhaps because of the similarities to my own marriage with Belgian author Philip Coppens. He wrote non-fiction, I wrote fiction, both out of a shared passion for ancient mysteries. Our paths felt parallel.

When Theresa first registered for one of my spiritual pilgrimage journeys, this one to Sacred France and an itinerary in the footsteps of Mary Magdalene, I was really excited. I was also a little intimidated. Theresa was, as the French would say, *formidable*. I wasn't sure what to expect from this woman who I admired for her intellect and achievements. I need not have worried. Theresa Crater was warm and kind and surprisingly reserved in the group. She held back and observed, yet with that kind of watchful interest which told me she wasn't missing a thing. Over the course of our pilgrimage we were able to spend more time together and a friendship developed between us. I adored her subtle yet sharp wit, and I was beginning to see just how deep and profound she was in her life and experiences.

The itinerary brought our group to the heart of Cathar Country in the French Pyrenees, a dramatically beautiful place with a rich and often tragic history. The Cathars were a medieval sect of Christians who practiced the Way of Love and did not acknowledge the supremacy of the Roman Church. The pope disapproved, and a brutal campaign was launched against the Cathars as heretics – a crusade which lasted over 100 years and caused the massacre of hundreds of thousands of innocent people in France and Italy. On our final day of our pilgrimage, we were visiting one of these Cathar locations. It is a subtle yet profound place; not famous, like the site of the terrible massacre at Montsegur, not legendary like the mysterious treasure village of Rennes le Chateau. This is a place of depth and beauty which whispers rather than screams.

It became clear to me that Theresa Crater heard the whisper of this place. I watched it happen in her, although she did not express much outwardly at the time. Later she would confide in me that the impact of this place had moved her to the point of transformation. I suppose in the end, I was not surprised that Theresa had such an altering energetic experience there. I had one as well over 20 years earlier. When I bring people to this particular place, I pay close attention to who is most moved by it as I always know that these are "my" people – people who respond to this same type of energy which has influenced my life and my own journey.

When I was asked to write the introduction to this book, I said yes immediately. I had to read it first, of course, but I was already clear that whatever Theresa would write would be something that would add great value to the conversation of spiritual awakenings. I was delighted from the very first page. I jumped in to her story of life as a follower of the legendary Maharishi Mahesh Yogi. This was iconic stuff. It was both fun and fascinating to have a glimpse into that rarified world which impacted so many on their spiritual journeys.

But it was when I arrived at the second awakening, and the story of Max the Crystal Skull, that I jumped out of my chair. Theresa and I had never talked about Max, and I had no idea that he was so important in her history. That same day, Theresa posted a photo of herself with Max on social media – and I replied with an almost identical photo of myself with Max taken a few years later. Here was another place where my new friend and I had a strong intersection. I laughed with delight as I read Theresa's story of Max the matchmaker. My own story with Max was very similar. I first met Max in the early stages of divorce from my first husband, and yet he told me that new love was coming very soon. I told him I didn't want it! I wasn't ready and I wasn't looking for it. Max said it didn't matter, it was happening and I should be ready. I remember it so clearly, because I thought it was somewhat shocking that a large chunk of crystal was not only forecasting my love life, but then he went on to name Philip Coppens as my future partner! And, just as with Theresa and Stephen, Max the Crystal Skull was absolutely right in his assessment. Philip and I married and remained inseparable until his untimely death in 2012. I am pleased to report that Max and his "keeper" Joann are still very dear friends and I still count Max as one of my spiritual teachers.

As for the third awakening in this book, which transpires in Cathar country, I am truly honored that I was a part of it in some way. I have been bringing people to this part of France for almost 20 years and have watched while that sacred land works on the cellular level of those pilgrims who are open to the experience. It is always a privilege to witness an awakening or a transformation, and Theresa's profound experience was meaningful for me.

I am proud to say that Theresa Crater is now someone I call a friend and a soul sister, and without a doubt is one of "my" people.

I look forward to the possibility of sharing more awakenings with her in the future, somewhere on this beautiful planet. May you be inspired by her journey, her wit, and her wisdom in pursuit of your own awakenings.

Kathleen McGowan
Luxor, Egypt 2022

Preface

I GOT A LOT OF ENCOURAGEMENT AND NUDGES to write this book from people, even from guides who would walk up to me in meditation and hand me a book. I only wished I could read it! A very talented psychic told me my angels were waiting for it and that the contents would be a lot of what we'd been talking about. I still doubted, though. Who am I to write such a book? I have friends who have mind-blowing experiences and are way more advanced than I am. I'm a toddler compared to many people. That's when I realized maybe that was the reason.

I'm an ordinary, everyday mystic who brushes her teeth and meditates twice a day. I have a lot of thoughts in meditation. Everybody does, by the way. I also teach meditation, and one of the important lessons is not to put emphasis on experiences. We meditate to heal our bodies and release stress through the deep rest it provides. We meditate to clear our minds and use our full mental potential. Meditation smooths out our emotions and heals deep wounds and traumas. Sometimes we need outside help with that. I know I did. We meditate for the world, for humanity, for the four-legged and winged-ones, for the biosphere, for Mother Gaia, for rapport with the larger galaxy, so humans can walk in harmony, not bring destruction.

Every day, I sit to meditate and for the most part, it's pretty ordinary. Of course, everybody loves those flashy meditations or the ones when we drop into deep silence and peace. The ones with lots of thoughts are just as valuable, believe it or not. I loved these flashes of enlightenment, though. They kept me going. They showed me I was making progress. But it is the everyday practice, sometimes slog, of meditation and action that is the backbone of spiritual growth. I can see, though, that I've grown steadily over the years. I'm more peaceful. My intuition is sharper. I can bring things to me more easily. Guidance is clearer.

I hope you enjoy this book because that's why I'm sharing these experiences. For everybody to know that the natural human condition is enlightenment and if I can make progress toward that state, then you most definitely can, too.

Theresa Crater
Boulder, CO 2022

Just sit there right now
Don't do a thing
Just rest.

For your separation from God,
From love,
Is the hardest work in this world.

Let me bring you trays of food
And something
That you like to
Drink.

You can use my soft words
As a cushion
For your
Head.

~ Hafiz[1] ~

---

[1] Hafiz, "A Cushion for Your Head," *The Gift*. Translated by Daniel Ladinsky, Penguin, 1999, 183.

Introduction

WE LOOKED INTO EACH OTHER'S eyes and burst out laughing. We laughed long and full at the delightful joke of it all. About how one piece of infinity came to another piece of infinity, asking to be made infinite. Asking in desperation, out of a crying need, in deep pain. And the joke was not only that this piece of infinity wanting so desperately to be infinite already was. But that I could not even have been searching, could not have even conceived infinity, if I hadn't already been exactly what I was looking for.

This is the story of the three awakenings I've experienced so far in my life. That "so far" is the same as saying "fingers crossed for more." All three were completely unexpected. They came out of the blue. They did not last, but after the first one I knew such a state of consciousness was possible.

In this book, I often refer to them as samadhis. Samadhi is a Sanskrit word that means *total self-connectedness*. Many people are familiar with this idea, and many have experienced it. The literal translation is *balanced intellect* or still mind. When the individual mind is still, it sees the universal consciousness that is its source. It recognizes that, in fact, it **is** that universal consciousness. Samadhi is conscious unity with the Divine.

Growing up, I never knew anything like this could happen. It just wasn't on my map of possibilities. I'm an ordinary person. Yes, I've been meditating for fifty-one years, but anybody can meditate. Yes, I was born into a psychic family, but I think all humans have intuitive abilities that get pushed down when we grow up in a culture that denies their existence.

As a child, I wanted a horse. Every time I had the opportunity to make a wish, every time I saw a falling star, found a four-leaf clover, or blew out my birthday candles, I wished for a horse. Yet I never believed these wishes would actually accomplish anything. I never believed I'd get a horse, but I did. When I was thirteen, my parents gave me Duke, a tall, leggy mixed thoroughbred/gated bay. The deal was I had to work at the stables cleaning stalls and feeding the horses at night to pay for his room and board. He was also used in riding lessons for the girls at Salem Academy and College. But I had a horse.

This gave me pause. Maybe all my wishes over the years had made a difference. As a teenager, I listened to Dr. King and marched for civil rights, desiring the end of racism and violence, and the growth of equality. I marched against the Vietnam War, wanting world peace. I wanted to be free and went off to college where I met new friends. Some of us learned to meditate together. We found some hints of human possibilities beyond what any of us had been taught so far. I pursued these possibilities with a passion.

I'm an ordinary person, but by now, just into my seventh decade, I've had many experiences that weren't on the 'map' I was given as a child, experiences that are available to everyone. It might take some work, some meditation, some clearing out of trauma—but the Divine is there beneath it all and accessible to everyone.

Humanity is searching for an answer, even the most satisfied among us. We feel a longing for something that we struggle to articulate. At some point in our lives, many of us embark on a serious search for our origin, our spiritual home, our secure and certain connection—to inner peace, to rightness and balance, to wholeness.

We search out there, outside ourselves, to reconnect. We look in the world, in other people, in books and scriptures, in spiritual teachers, in a relationship, in marriage. But the problem is that what we are looking for is inside. It is the very thing we use to search with. It is our own consciousness, which makes the whole business a bit tricky. Our own awareness contains the answers we seek, the wholeness we yearn for, the balance and self-knowing that we want so desperately. Eventually, in one life or another, we find it and when we do, we discover that we never left.

MEDITATION

1

THE FIRST TIME I EXPERIENCED SAMADHI, I was sitting in front of Maharishi Mahesh Yogi in a ski resort in the town of Courchevel, France. The year was 1975. The Transcendental Meditation (TM) movement rented hotels for teacher training and advanced meditation courses in the off-season. It was fall and we were tucked under Mount Blanc, the highest mountain in the French Alps. The snow had just arrived and Theresa Crater provided a satisfying crunch under our feet at night.

I had come to plead for Maharishi to allow me to continue my teacher training class. Being a TM teacher was my life's mission. At least, I thought so at the time. The women in an advanced course where I was working as a staff member had finagled a way for me to have a private audience with him. His attendants were not happy about it. In fact, they stood arguing about it with one of my co-conspirators outside the meeting room. Another one of my friends gave me a shove into the room where Maharishi sat on his dais. When he beckoned me forward, his staff couldn't exactly contradict him.

After my stumbling request to continue the teacher training course, Maharishi gave me his answer, one I didn't like. He didn't just open the door and say, "Walk on through." He told me to talk to the course office. I knew what they'd say. I'd already talked to them, several times in fact. I was certain the door had just been slammed in my face and I'd never become a TM teacher. I sat there, deflated and disappointed. Then I asked myself if I was going to accept the answer of the man I then thought of as my spiritual master or if I was going to argue with him. I surrendered to the situation. I remembered I'd always wanted to look into Maharishi's eyes. They seemed vast, oceanic, containing the wisdom I yearned for. At least they seemed that way on the TV screen where I usually saw him.

I looked up at him. He was clearly amused, his eyes twinkling. When our eyes met, something happened. He looked into me and when he did, he saw all of me. And then so did I. I experienced for the first time that I was not simply a person called Theresa who was begging to go to some course so I could realize my infinite consciousness. I already was infinite. In fact, I couldn't have wanted to become infinite if I wasn't already the universal consciousness I so desperately sought. We both burst out laughing at the big joke of it all.

I went away knowing that I would probably lose this expanded state. That I would forget and fall back into yearning to become what I already was.

But I'd had my first taste of enlightenment.

What the heck was going on? How had I ended up at the feet of Maharishi, in a ski hotel of all places, experiencing this elevated state of consciousness?

Maharishi Mahesh Yogi
(Vernon Barnes Ph.D., 1978). CC BY 3.0

I completed the first three months of the TM teacher training course the year before this encounter in another ski resort town, this one in Livigno, Italy. We watched videos of Maharishi in a large rec room converted into a lecture hall. We ate lunch while watching the Italian ski team train for the Olympics by skiing down the barely covered slopes and taking off in brightly colored, mini parachutes when they hit the rocky cliff. It seemed nuts to me. They might have thought the same of us. After lunch, we walked around the little town exploring for about an hour. The rest of the time we spent in our rooms meditating.

Livigno, Italy
(Sentiero 113 – Livigno 09). CC BY 2.0

The schedule started with just one session consisting of prescribed yoga asanas, a form of pranayama or special breathing, and meditation. This was called a round. After a little while, we added a round in the morning and another in the afternoon. Soon we are doing "three and three," three rounds in the morning, and three in the afternoon.

Because this much meditation tends to make people are little spacy or unearth deep stress, we were supposed to never go anywhere alone. We had a buddy system, and it seemed natural that my life partner, whom I'm calling Beth here, would be mine. We'd been involved with TM since we both started meditating. I was pursuing my life dream with her. I was in paradise. Okay, the Italian Alps, but still…

One day early in the course, the leaders called Beth and me to a special meeting. They informed us that our center leaders back home had set a condition on our acceptance to the course. We had to be separated.

This came as a major shock. Beth and I had served as the unofficial TM center in Greensboro, North Carolina, soon after I started meditating. I was hooked from the start. After learning on my own, I attended Beth's four days of TM instruction, then we attended all the four-day courses for new meditators. That's where we learned the Vedic teachings about higher states of consciousness. Many people are familiar with these ideas nowadays, but when I was twenty, it was all new to me.

Unity Consciousness was considered enlightenment in the TM tradition. In Unity, the individual mind is united with the One Consciousness behind all creation and that person perceives that everything and everyone is that One Consciousness. This is not just an idea, but a concrete experience. This is what I experienced sitting with Maharishi—samadhi. But my connection to the One Consciousness didn't last long. When we reach full enlightenment, the experience never fades. This is the Vedic teaching, and you'll find the same teaching in other traditions as well.

I had a taste of enlightenment that evening in Courchevel, but I paid a very high price for it. Was the price worth it? That's a very hard question to answer. Unity is the answer to all questions, the healing of all wounds, and the complete balancing of the personality as it rests in the universal mind. This is what I experienced at that moment. What price is too high for that?

And yet, the price was too high because what happened to me and to Beth was based in ignorance and prejudice. This group was supposed to be bringing enlightenment to the world.

This was a complete contradiction and yet all of it seemed true to me.

I was the first to be initiated into the TM technique, much to Beth's surprise. I didn't remember at the time that I'd heard about TM when I was sixteen, way back in 1966, which seemed like a long time to me then.

The Beatles had discovered Maharishi in London and increased his fame by going to his ashram in India and learning to meditate. I was a fan at the time and followed them closely. Then came a vinyl record album of two talks by Maharishi. I bought the record and listened to the high, lilting voice of the serene man with appropriately longish hair whose picture graced the cover.

Maharishi Mahesh Yogi, the Beatles' spiritual teacher speaks to the youth of the world on Love and the untapped source of power that lies within, the back cover declared. I liked that he directed his message to us, the young generation that I felt certain was special. Destined to do great things and save the world. I'd told my mother this when I was about five. She laughed at me. "We all think that when we're young, Theresa."

I sat in the living room in a rocking chair in front of our brick fireplace and played Maharishi's LP on the big stereo the size of a credenza in those days. Afterward, I remember closing my eyes and just being quiet, imagining this was the Transcendental Deep Meditation described on the record. It wasn't, but I did this for a while, just sitting quietly.

In Greensboro five years later, I got the chance to learn for real. The year was 1971. Beth and I walked across the University of North Carolina at Greensboro campus, enjoying the scent of gardenias permeating the close August evening. We were headed to an introductory lecture on TM held in the stone and glass Lutheran Center. We walked through the foyer covered in greenhouse-like windows filled with potted plants. Beth opened one of the metal doors to the large open room they used for events and took a seat in the back row. I sat beside her and looked around the room, waiting for the lecture to start. We didn't know anyone else there except Eileen, who was leaning over a projector with a small, blond man who looked vaguely familiar. They were talking in low voices.

"It should work now. Try it," Eileen said.

Beth sat next to me, staring down at her hands and occasionally shuffling her feet around. She was a large woman with a crown of curls that she had allowed to do as they pleased instead of spending hours trying to flatten them into the acceptable pageboy of her high school days. At this moment, she looked like a lost St. Bernard puppy.

The projector whined and squeaked. "No, it's just not working."

Eileen and the blond man began rethreading the machine. Their patience annoyed me. I was myself bad with mechanical devices, and it irritated me when people wouldn't stop fiddling with a broken machine and simply admit that the thing had won.

I leaned close and asked Beth, "Don't you know how to run a projector?"

Beth glanced up at me but didn't reply.

"Well, I may have to just talk without the film," I heard the man say, "but I'd really prefer to show it."

He sent an appraising glance around the room. "We're having a small problem with the projector. It'll just be a minute."

He wore a blue suit, red tie, and loafers. Odd, in the 1970s counterculture, but the pants were too short, so I was willing to overlook it.

"Didn't you say you ran the projector in high school?" I poked Beth in the side.

"I don't know how to operate that kind," Beth said, still staring at her hands.

I gave up. Beth had that bull-in-a-pasture look about her, and I knew she couldn't be moved.

The blond man walked to the front of the circle of chairs, then stood facing us, his hands folded in front of him. First, he smiled and looked around at each of the people in the room. "I'm glad that you all have come here tonight. My name is Johnny and I'm a teacher of meditation. The projector seems to be broken, so I'm afraid you'll just have me to listen to tonight."

A few people chuckled.

"How many of you know someone who meditates?"

I raised my hand eagerly. A few other hands went up. Beth carefully studied her shoes.

"Great. Actually, meditators are the best advertisers of the technique. Usually, people start because their friends do it. Because they've seen some changes."

He paused. "In fact, how many of your friends told you 'Don't listen to a word he says. Start anyway?'"

Laughter rolled across the room and more hands went up. People began to relax. I sat back and listened, watching Johnny's pink hands wave in the air. Suddenly, I remembered that I had met

7

him before at Eileen's apartment. Beth and I had stopped by on an afternoon walk and tapped on the back door. We waited what seemed like a long time.

"Eileen?" I knocked louder.

Finally, Eileen opened the door and we walked in. Her long print skirt rustled gently as she silently shut the door behind her.

"Hi," she whispered, "what's up?"

"We just came to say 'hello,'" my voice dropped to a whisper in mid-sentence when Eileen's finger went up to her lips. "What's going on?"

"Johnny is teaching meditation here today," Eileen said.

We stood awkwardly in the kitchen, then sat around the table. Eileen sat hugging her legs to her, one hand wrapped around a mug, looking out the window with a quiet smile on her face. She seemed content and unreachable like she was sitting on top of some high mountain looking down on the valley, thinking how beautiful it was from this distance. The wind chimes on her porch sounded faintly, giving body to the silence.

"And you don't want to work on the committee anymore," I said as if out of the blue. Last year Eileen had been the head of the student organization that had almost shut down the school over the Vietnam War. It was a statement rather than a question, but Eileen understood exactly what I meant.

"No, I don't want to do that kind of political work anymore." Eileen looked at me steadily. "I think I can get more done with meditating."

A short man in a three-piece blue suit and stocking feet stuck his head around the corner and gestured for Eileen. She looked at him and nodded, then said to us, "I need to go back in. Let's talk about it again sometime. Or why don't you go to a lecture and hear about it for yourself?"

So, here I was. Johnny began drawing something on the chalkboard, explaining a concept. "The mind settles down to a state of silence," he said, illustrating silence with a straight line. "Thought arises from this quiet state of mind, small at first, subtle." He emphasized this last word with a glance over his shoulder, then he drew a small circle. "Then it gets more concrete, more gross." He drew larger circles.

I didn't know what this had to do with meditating, but a sense of palpable quiet, a deep peace, was creeping up on me. I felt almost humble before it.

Johnny stood in front of the chalkboard and faced the audience again. I'd missed something. He put down the chalk and asked, "Are there any questions?"

"How do you start?" I asked.

Johnny beamed.

Beth frowned.

I was a bit surprised as well, but it was more a recognition of a feeling I'd had since that day at Eileen's, that there was something important happening here. I knew I should learn to meditate, that it was my next step. But it was an instinctive knowledge, like a cat knowing to lick her newborn kitten. Nothing I could explain.

"There are two requirements to begin meditating. One is that you attend all the classes we offer in the first two weeks, six in all. And second, that you refrain from using all recreational drugs prior to learning."

A rustle went through the room. Johnny raised his hand. "We don't take a moral position on the use of drugs. This is purely a physiological consideration. Drugs have a powerful effect on the body and mind. After all, if they didn't, we wouldn't use them."

One man with long tangled hair and bare feet snorted loudly at this, then turned red. Everyone laughed. It was the early 1970s, after all.

Johnny went on, "What we've found after a lot of experience is that people have a clearer experience if they've refrained from using drugs for two weeks. Maharishi, our main teacher, initiated people in San Francisco for five years before he made this requirement."

A dark-haired woman sitting to my right raised her hand. "Does this cost anything?"

"Yes," Johnny said. "The cost for the program is $35 if you are a college student and $50 for working adults."

Beth squirmed around a little at this. I was surprised, but it didn't seem too high.

"Are there more questions?" Johnny asked. No one said anything. "Thank you all for coming to hear about meditation tonight. I hope you've enjoyed the lecture. Those who are interested in starting to meditate should stay behind. If you are interested in being notified of upcoming lectures, please sign our mailing list. Thank you." He walked to the back of the room.

People began talking and moving around, getting backpacks and purses, discussing the talk. I sat still, feeling strangely peaceful and silent. Beth scooted closer and leaned her head toward me. "So, you really want to do this thing?" she asked.

I nodded.

"Why?"

I lifted my hand and took a breath, searching for words.

Before I could find any, Beth went on, "Did you understand that stuff about thoughts being like bubbles? And that crap about physics? I hate pseudoscientific stuff like that. It's like they have to pretend to be scientific to be acceptable."

I looked at Beth's face. She was scowling, her forehead wrinkled, her jaw set, eyes hooded. "What are you so upset about?"

Beth propped one leg over her other knee and started sticking the ends of her shoelaces into the holes of her sneakers. "I'm not upset. Why do you want to do this stuff, anyway?"

"Because I feel like it's the right thing for me. It's nothing about what he said. It's just that I feel like I should do it. I don't know how to explain it. I'll just see what it's like."

Beth leaned her head sideways and said nothing for a while. At last, she heaved a sigh and let her foot slide to the floor. "OK, but I'm not doing it. Everybody's always trying to save the Jews, and I'm fine the way I am, thank you. And you have to pay for it yourself."

Her reaction was completely out of left field. I reached over and took her hand. "Okay, everything will be fine. You'll see."

Johnny returned to the front of the room and smiled at the six remaining people. "So, all of you want to start next weekend?"

"No," Beth said immediately.

He paused. "Well, this information is for those people who know they are ready to start. Would you like to wait outside?"

I could almost hear the wheels turning. *Now comes the part where he tells the real truth.* Beth's gaze darted over to the curtains. I imagined that Beth was half expecting Johnny to draw them closed, take out a pendulum, and say, *"You are getting very sleepy."*

"Can't I stay?" she asked, setting her shoulders.

"Certainly," Johnny answered. He began passing out forms. Everyone bent quietly over their papers. The questions were standard at first—name, address, age.

I pondered 'marital status,' then marked single.

Beth read over her shoulder. "Why do they want to know if you've ever been to a shrink?"

"I don't know." I didn't like answering these questions, either, but she knew I wanted to do this and nothing was really going to stop me at this point.

Beth raised her voice and asked, "Why do you need to know if people have ever gone to psychologists?"

"If people are currently doing therapy when they start meditating, we like for their therapist to know so they can better understand any changes."

Beth pondered this.

"When you finish filling out your forms, please bring them up one by one to talk with me privately for a few minutes, and then I'll see you next Saturday."

✰✰✰

The morning sun pushed its way through the thin bamboo shades and fell in strips, catching the curved leaf of the spathiphyllum, the pile of abandoned blue jeans and tee shirts, and the block print bedspread. Dust motes floated serenely in the morning light, settling on the thickly painted black pine dresser from Goodwill. Penelope, the calico, let out a soft meep and crawled up onto my stomach, turning and kneading before she lay down. Penelope purred as I stroked her pastel grays and peaches, then reached out a padded paw to touch the other cat she saw reflected in my eye.

I turned my head away from the paw to watch Beth sleeping, Artemis curled just above her head like a black fur hat. I stole a glance at the alarm. It would soon go off, and Beth would roll out of bed and head out for the biology lab for her Saturday work shift.

I would be heading off to learn to meditate. I reviewed in my mind what I needed to do. Get fruit and flowers. I had a list somewhere of what Johnny had asked each person to bring. First, there was to be some ceremony, then I got my own mantra.

The alarm buzzed. Penelope ran. Artemis blinked. Beth turned over with a loud moan and hit the button, silencing the clock. Everything was still for a minute. Then

Beth peeked out from under the covers. "I hate working on Saturday."

I moved closer and put my head on Beth's shoulder. Then pushed a little.

"Move over. I'm on the crack."

Beth shifted her weight slightly. "I've got to tie these mattresses together sometime," she said sleepily. We had two twin mattresses we'd picked up from Goodwill and put them together on the floor.

"What time do you go to work?"

"From eleven to three."

I raised my head and looked at Beth. "Then why the alarm?"

"I wanted to get some things done."

"God, you're just like my mother." My mother was an early riser and considered it a point of moral superiority over my father and me who slept in. "I'm going to start meditating today," I said.

"Oh, that. Well, I hope you like it. What time?" Beth yawned.

"The guy who's teaching me will pick me up at 11:30 or so. I'm the first one. I have to get flowers and stuff."

"There are some beautiful roses growing in the old ladies' yard down the alley. Let's go snitch some."

"Great." I snuggled deeper, pleased Beth was going to help.

We showered and dressed, then snuck out to the old ladies' garden where we picked coral roses that grew near the back fence. We were curious about the two old women who looked like they were in their seventies. All summer long they worked in their garden in long flowered dresses, bib aprons, and large-brimmed straw hats. Beth and I made up stories about them. They were long-time lovers who had been founders of this new women's college or at least among the first graduates. They had moved into the surrounding country and now continued to live as they always had on their half-acre as the town grew up around them.

Besides their roses, we found sweet peas that had taken over the fence in the back yard of another house and grown into the alley, hanging in profusion, still a deep purple. We gathered wild daises and other flowers that were lovely but nameless to us. I bought a packet of white handkerchiefs with little flowers embroidered on them from a store just beside the hamburger joint one block from our apartment.

"Are you going to learn that TM?" the saleslady asked.

Beth and I looked at each other, surprised. "Uh, yes. How did you know?"

"We sell a lot of handkerchiefs these days and most people say they're going to learn to meditate. Used to be the girls would keep them tucked in their belt or in their handbag."

"Times have changed," I said.

"They certainly have." But she didn't seem too upset about it. Thinking back, I imagine she was glad for the business.

We went back to our apartment. Beth wrapped the stems of my flowers in layers of wet paper towels, put the bottom in a plastic bag, and ran off to work.

By 11:30, I sat on the front steps with a handful of summer flowers waiting for Johnny to pick me up. I shifted out of the hot sun, an apple, a peach, and a banana in a brown paper sack in my lap, my flowers sticking out the top. With my corsage, I felt as close to a bride as I thought I was ever likely to be.

Johnny was almost half an hour late. When he showed up, he jumped out of the car and waved his hand for me to jump in. "I'm late. I got lost."

I settled into the front seat of the Pinto.

"Now," he said, "do you know where this place is?" He handed me a map drawn on the back of an envelope. No GPS for us by then. I recognized the general area of the city they were heading for and started giving directions.

Once underway he seemed to relax. "Those are beautiful flowers. Where did you get them?"

"I picked them." I took a sniff.

Johnny smiled. "It's nice to have wildflowers. Most people buy them."

"In August?"

"Yes, can you believe it? What do you do?"

"I'm a student."

"Right. What are you studying?"

"Sociology. I was a music major, but it seemed impractical all of a sudden."

He turned a corner. "What are you going to do when you graduate?"

"I don't know. Probably social work, but . . ." I hesitated.

His slightly buggy blue eyes were busy searching for street signs. He wore a tan suit today, slightly wrinkled. I wondered why he didn't wear jeans, the universal outfit of the times.

"I don't know what to do really. The world's a mess, you know, and I'd like to do something about it. But they just don't pay you for that. Social work's a compromise, of course. Some people think we should just sit back and let things get really bad so people will revolt."

He smiled.

"But I don't want to spend my life in a place where things keep getting worse and worse."

Johnny said cryptically, "Well, we'll see how you feel after today."

When we arrived, Johnny introduced me to the woman whose apartment this was, saying she was a new meditator, but I didn't catch her name. The woman and Johnny buzzed around getting things ready while I sat in the front corner of the living room, listening to the hustle and bustle in the back of the apartment.

In a few more minutes, the woman walked hesitantly into the front room, half smiling at me, then said, "Johnny will be ready in a minute. How were you going to pay today?"

I reached for my pack, pulled out a blue vinyl wallet, and handed her three new ten dollar bills and a more rumpled five. The woman wrote out a receipt which I had no idea what to do with, then disappeared into the kitchen. I talked to Beth recently, meaning in 2022, and she still has her receipt from September 1971. Amazing.

I was just beginning to get impatient when the woman reappeared carrying my flowers and fruit elegantly laid out in a wicker basket. I took a breath in surprise. She smiled, then asked me to remove my shoes. After I had unlaced my tennis shoes and piled them in the corner, the woman handed me the basket, then started down the hall. I followed, holding my offerings in an almost formal procession. When she reached the last door, she knocked then stepped aside.

Johnny opened the door and a clean, sweet smell drifted out. He carefully took the basket piled high with flowers. I walked into the room, trying to take in everything at once. Immediately to the right was a table draped in folds of white. I caught the gleam of small brass dishes and the yellow glow of a candle. Johnny motioned toward one of two folding chairs sitting in the middle of the room facing the draped table. I sat down and my eyes were immediately caught by the stern gaze of an old Indian man looking out from a large gold frame. He was different from the picture in the newspaper ad. He sat erect draped in orange robes on a gilded throne surrounded by flowers.

Before we could completely take each other in, Johnny started talking. "Do you understand what we are going to do today?"

I nodded, then glanced around. On both sides and behind me, this was an ordinary bedroom with a low single bed pushed against the back wall, now spread with Johnny's papers. A bookshelf and dresser stood on either side of the room. In front, the room changed completely. There stood what could only be described as an altar.

". . . and you don't have to know the ceremony I'm going to perform. Just watch it. Do you have any questions?" Johnny looked at me and waited.

"Uh," I glanced at him, down at the papers in his hands, recognizing the form she had filled out last week at the lecture, and wondered what he had just said. "So, what is this ceremony about anyway?"

By the look on his face, I could see that this was what he had just finished explaining. "I mean," I hunched my shoulders slightly, "you said it isn't religious, right?"

Johnny nodded. "Right. It's a ceremony to honor the line of teachers who have kept this wisdom and passed it on through the ages. Remember that this meditation comes from a different culture. In India, there's much more respect for teachers and older people. So, what to us might appear to be worship is really an expression of respect."

I looked up at the older man sitting in his frame. He looked quite comfortable surrounded by small shining brass dishes and the reds, violets, and yellows of my offerings, like he was used to this sort of thing. I nodded at Johnny.

"So, any other questions before we begin?"

I shook my head.

"Okay. Please stand beside me." He motioned for me to get up, then pointed to the picture of the old Indian man I'd been staring at all this time.

"This is His Holiness Swami Bramananda Saraswati, the Shankaracharya of Jyoti Math. He was Maharishi's teacher. Today his picture will represent all the teachers through the ages who have kept this wisdom alive." He turned and faced Guru Dev, as I later learned he was called, bowed his head, and closed his eyes for a minute.

A thin stream of smoke curled up from a stick of incense burning in a brass holder. The silence deepened. Johnny opened his eyes and began to sing. His voice was soft and rhythmic, but I couldn't understand the words. Then I realized he was singing in a different language and started to relax, drifting with his voice and the curling line of smoke rising from the altar. The moment detached itself from the usual expectations of a summer afternoon and rose like a glistening soap bubble from a child's blow ring, at once transparent and reflecting every color of the rainbow.

Johnny started to place things on the tray in front of the picture, a sweet pea blossom, grains of rice, more flowers, the apple. He dipped a coral rose into the dish of water, then sprinkled the offerings on the tray. Drops of liquid magnified the red skin of the fruit. His voice droned on pleasantly.

After a few minutes, he turned and gestured for me to give him the sweet peas I was holding. All his motions were soundless and flowed in slow motion. Nothing in the world existed except the things on this table and this ancient song. He placed the purple blooms on the tray with the rose he was holding, sank to his knees, and seemed to bow his head.

Surprised, I looked down to see what he was doing, but my eyes were caught by a subtle movement on the altar. On the tray surrounding the offerings was a crystalline topaz ball of light. I blinked, but it remained, a golden egg pulsating gently, as if it was breathing in and out. A clean stream flowed through my body. I could not imagine what was happening, but it felt very familiar.

Johnny stood, caught my attention, and began repeating a sound. He gestured with his hands that I was to repeat the sound with him. I began saying it slowly. He stopped. So did I. He gestured for me to continue. I said it again, glancing at him to see if I was pronouncing it correctly. He nodded. I tried it out a few more times, two round vowels that felt like a small boat going over a wave.

Johnny motioned for me to sit down and keep repeating the word. It was starting to slow down now and stretch out like someone in a warm bath. I was still whispering, but my eyes were closed. I wanted to stop saying the sound out loud, stop all motion. Just sit still and listen to it echo in my mind. I was barely whispering when Johnny finally said, "You can stop saying the mantra out loud now."

So, this is my mantra. The thought slipped by.

I stopped moving my lips and let the word go. It dropped softly, like a leaf, and settled somewhere deep inside, embedded in deep drifts of silence.

Johnny's voice floated across to me. "Open your eyes, please."

It wasn't so much that his voice sounded far away as that it seemed to exist in some different dimension and I could choose whether or not to respond.

"Open your eyes," he repeated in a soft tone.

I was amused that I had gone into a different world, then remembered that he was waiting for me to reply. I opened my eyes and looked at him.

"How was it?" he asked.

What a funny question, I thought.

I didn't know how to convey my experience to him. As I pondered this, he asked if I felt relaxed. This was such a small part of it, but I nodded. Trying to describe what had just happened seemed as inadequate as just saying something innocuous like, "it was fine," so that's what I said and sat marveling at the canyon between my experience and my words. But I had some faith that he understood my experience. After all, he meditated too. He had just taught me how. He'd been sitting in the same room, right beside me.

"Good. Now I'd like you to go into the next room and meditate for a little longer.

Someone will come and tell you when to stop. Then I'll answer your questions."

I followed him into the hall, glancing at the altar as I left. The only light left was the candle reflecting in the brass dishes. I walked down the hall, avoiding the woman's discreet but curious glance, not wanting to come out of this magical circle. I walked into the room the woman pointed out.

"Make yourself at home," she said. "You can sit anywhere you're comfortable. On the bed, in one of these chairs, or in the beanbag chair. That's my favorite one to meditate in." She smiled conspiratorially.

"Thanks." I shut the door, sank into the nearest chair, not even glancing around, and closed my eyes. For a while, I was completely absorbed by the soft pulse of the mantra, like the slow opening and closing of a butterfly's wings as it rests in the sun. Gradually other thoughts began to drift by and the outside world returned. Children's voices floated through the open window. I opened my eyes. The curtains lifted soundlessly in the breeze, filling the room with golden afternoon sunlight. I felt full, not needing to move, yet light. I was whole for the first time in my life. Whole, still, full. All sound and movement were ripples on the surface of a deep lake, moving but always staying the same.

So, I've found it at last.

The thought glided by quietly. I was surprised. I hadn't known I was looking for anything.

2

THIS EXPERIENCE HAD NOT BEEN on my map of possibilities. I'd never felt such deep peace, never experienced such a sense of rightness. I was hooked. I meditated regularly, although the profundity of that first time didn't repeat itself. Still, I felt better. Toward the end of August, Beth and our roommate Tom commented that I'd changed. "You're calmer," she said.

Tom agreed. "You don't get angry about things so easily."

I tried not to get defensive about this. I still had a way to go.

"You seem more self-contained. I'm going to learn," Beth declared. So she and another friend were initiated in September. Tom learned sometime, too. I can't recall which month. After that, Beth and I usually meditated together, sometimes with Tom and Rich, our other roommates. I attended Beth's four days of TM instruction, then we started attending all the four-day courses offered for new meditators.

We lived in an old clapboard house that used to be white and had been divided up into four apartments, two downstairs, one upstairs, and one in the converted garage out back. The woman who lived in the apartment adjacent to ours learned to meditate, then started dating the new TM teacher. The front doors of the ground floor apartments both opened out onto a large front porch, where Beth and I, and our neighbor and other assorted visitors, used to sit outside on warm evenings, gossiping and swatting mosquitoes. So, it naturally evolved that their house started functioning as the meditation center for Greensboro.

Eileen had new roommates and had taken up painting in earnest. The extra bedroom they'd used as the initiation room was now cluttered with easels, brushes, rags and all sorts of artistic paraphernalia. It was too much of a hassle to clean up every other Saturday morning for Johnny to teach meditation, so she conceded the honor to us. Tom and Rich had moved and we had extra room.

Both Beth and I wanted to become meditation teachers. The woman in the apartment adjacent to ours took a break from college and attended the teacher training course in Mallorca, Spain, but we decided to finish our degrees first. It never occurred to us we'd have any problems. No one had ever said a word to us about being lesbians or suggested this would be a problem for us in becoming teachers and representing the movement. We were solid meditators with a strong understanding of the teachings, and we'd helped the movement get established in our town.

At first, when we arrived at the first half of the teacher training course, all went well. As I described earlier, we were called into a meeting after the first few weeks of the course. In the hotel in Livigno, we waited in the broad-beamed lobby while the course leaders conferred. Finally, a little guy with a mustache who looked like Groucho Marx stepped out of the hotel manager's office and asked us to come inside. He gestured for us to find a seat, then turned back to the other course leaders who were still talking among themselves. We sat in two chairs near the window facing a large, cluttered desk where one of the teachers – let's call him Jack – sat scowling at papers.

After a minute, the man who had shown us in asked, "Do you need me? I can go take care of the water heater if you think you can handle these girls alone."

It was pointless to object to being called girls.

"Go ahead. I think the three of us can handle it." He looked at the other two teachers for confirmation. His wife, Melinda, and the teacher from the other hotel, Steve (not their real names), were with him. They both nodded.

"What do you think this is about?" Beth whispered.

I shrugged, starting to feel nervous.

Jack cleared his throat, then said, "Let's get straight to the point. We've been very busy getting the course underway, straightening out all the major problems, and have just begun to turn our attention to the individual ones."

I glanced at Beth out of the corner of my eye, but Beth was watching Jack carefully, arms folded across her stomach.

"It seems that you two have a conditional acceptance."

"A what?" I asked.

"Your acceptance depends on your meeting certain requirements."

"What requirements?" I asked. "We've completed all the volunteer work and the introductory course."

"It's nothing like that." Jack waved his hand.

"We weren't told anything about this. We just got a phone call, then a telegram to confirm our acceptance right before we left," Beth said.

"Your center told you nothing about this?" Melinda asked, her eyes widening. "No," I said.

Beth shook her head.

The three exchanged a quick glance, then Jack continued, "Well, your acceptance is based on the condition that the two of you attend separate courses—"

"What?" I stiffened.

"—and that you do not see each other for the remainder of the course."

"That's outrageous." Beth swept her hand in front of her to wipe away what Jack had just said.

"These are the conditions of your acceptance," he repeated.

"Wait a minute," I said.

"But, why?" Beth stuttered.

"Because of your relationship," Jack said.

"What about our relationship?" Beth's eyes narrowed.

"Well, certainly you don't need me to spell it out." Jack shrank back in his chair squeamishly.

Melinda leaned forward with a patronizing smile. "National said that you have a, uh, that you are, well, lesbians, and the organization cannot be represented by homosexuals."

We were silent for a long minute. Beth recovered first. "You can't accept us onto the course and then . . . we've been here for two weeks. You can't turn around and tell us we're not accepted when we're already here in the middle of the Alps."

"You are accepted," Jack said, "although I must admit that if it had been my center, I wouldn't have recommended you." He looked at Melinda and she nodded her agreement. Steve was studying his hands. "But your acceptance is conditional. If you wish to remain on the course, you must separate today and not see each other for the rest of the course. If you don't agree to do this, you must leave immediately."

"No," I said, more to stave off what was happening than to answer.

"Then you'll have to leave the course," Jack said.

"No." This was an answer.

"So, you're going to separate," Jack said.

I opened my mouth to say something, but Melinda interrupted. "You really should think about what you are doing. This organization will not allow homosexuals to become teachers. We must be represented by the best people in society if we are going to be taken seriously. Surely you understand this." She tried to look neutral. "The organization will never allow lesbians to become teachers."

I felt like someone was holding my head under water. Beth gripped the arm of the chair, her knuckles white.

"Never is a very long time." Steve's quiet voice floated across the room.

Melinda blinked and looked at Steve like she'd forgotten he was there. "Yes, well, don't you agree?" she asked him.

He looked at her evenly. "All I know is that never is a long time. It's not up to us to say who will become teachers and who won't."

"Well, of course it is. That's what these courses are all about," Melinda said.

"Look," Jack fixed his gaze back on Beth and me, "this is not a moral judgment. It's not up to us to tell you if being a, uh, homosexual is right. What we are telling you is that to teach effectively, we have to go by the rules and morality of the country we are teaching in. And we can't have homosexuals representing the knowledge." He held his hands up and sat back as if the discussion was at an end.

"No one's going to know we're lesbians," Beth said. "We aren't going to be out when we're teaching."

"We know you're lesbians," Melinda said.

"Well, of course you know. That's because we told the people at the center and, I guess, they told you. If we hadn't told you, you wouldn't have known." I felt like I was instructing first grade. "We'll be discrete when we're teachers."

"If we found out, other people will find out," Melinda insisted.

"No, that's not true," Beth said. "Look, we were open with the teachers in our town because they were—" she closed her eyes for a second and took a breath "—we thought they were our friends. I mean, they stayed in our spare room when they came to town. We ran the center from our house. Why didn't they tell us then?"

"They allowed you to have courses in your home?" Jack was clearly scandalized.

"If we found out, other people will," Melinda repeated.

"You found out because we told you." I strained to control myself. I'd been in this organization long enough to know that overt anger would get us nowhere. "There are plenty of lesbians in the world in respected, professional positions, and no one knows they are gay."

Melinda was shaking her head.

"It's true." My voice rose in spite of my efforts. "There are lots of lesbians on the faculty at the college we attended. The public doesn't know that. It doesn't mean nobody knows. Their friends know. They know how to be discrete at appropriate times." I was a swimmer caught in a powerful undertow.

"I don't believe there really are as many homosexuals on the university faculty as you think." Melinda sounded like a psychiatric social worker. "But it's irrelevant. We are talking about the organization here. We are more important than some state university." She looked at Jack. "I just don't think homosexuals can ever become meditation teachers."

"What is this all about?" Beth interrupted angrily, her voice loud. "We've been on the course for two weeks. We are now meditating four hours a day. We're not supposed to be making any major decisions. You won't even let us go to town alone. And you call us in here to tell us we can never be teachers?"

"Well, unfortunately, it's not that simple," Jack said sarcastically. "What we are here to tell you is that you must choose between the terms of your acceptance to the course, to separate for the next two and a half months, or leave."

I felt like I was sinking, but Beth was getting angrier. "Why weren't we told this before we got here? If we'd known this, then I would have kept my job and stayed home while Theresa came to the whole six months." She glanced over and I nodded. I didn't know if I really agreed, but it seemed like the politic thing to do under the circumstances.

Beth barged ahead. "This is unacceptable. You want us to separate or leave. What if we leave? Will you refund us the full course fee and all travel expenses?"

Jack and Melinda looked at each other.

Steve suddenly got involved. "That seems like the only fair thing to do. It was the organization's mistake not to tell them the conditions of their acceptance. The least we can do is refund their money."

Jack said quickly, "Well Steve, I think that we'll have to go by organizational policy here. Full refunds are not available this late into the course. Maybe—"

"I'm not going to leave." My voice was quiet and shaky but held an undertone of granite.

Beth looked at me, astonished.

I stared down at my hands. "I have to be a teacher. There's nothing else for me to do."

Beth made a choking sound, but I pressed on. "I've known I was going to be a teacher from the day I was initiated. We're going to stay."

"Then you agree to separate?" Jack asked.

"No," I said in the same quiet voice.

"You have no choice. If you stay, you have to stay separately."

"No. We won't do that either."

"Look," Melinda reasoned. "It would be an ugly scene. If you refuse to do as national asks, then we have no choice but to turn you out of the lecture hall and out of meals. It would be very uncomfortable for everyone."

"I want to talk to Maharishi about this." I continued to stare at my hands, refusing to meet the row of faces in front of me.

"That's impossible," Jack said.

"Why?" Beth challenged him.

"The decision has been made. We can't bother Maharishi about this."

"I want to talk to him," I repeated. "We won't leave until we've talked to
Maharishi."

Jack was flushed. "We can force you to leave. Kick you out of your rooms, throw your stuff out on the street." Through clenched teeth he said, "We don't want dykes in our organization."

I turned halfway around in my seat as if I'd been struck. Beth rose then sat down again abruptly.

"Jack, let's not get carried away," Steve said in a shocked tone, but Jack ignored him.

"These are the conditions of your admission," he said, eyes narrowed. "You either have to separate or leave. Since you refuse to separate, we must force you to leave. And that's probably for the best, because you should never have been accepted in the first place."

"Then what am I supposed to do with my life?" I screamed. I jumped up and ran out the door.

"Theresa, wait," Steve called after me.

"We have to settle this," Jack shouted.

"Leave her alone," Beth snarled behind me.

My shoulders were heaving. People in the lobby turned to stare. Someone walked up to me and reached out to comfort me, but I shook my head and, sobbing, broke into a run.

The course leaders kept arguing with us and we kept insisting on talking to Maharishi. They said we had to leave the course, but we could see him on our way home. We agreed, but nobody made any arrangements for this to happen. When Daniel, a man from Maharishi's staff arrived to check on the progress of the course, we all met again. He agreed to take our request to the master himself, so we settled down to wait. We were still living in the same suite together. Still attending the same lectures.

One evening during a lecture, I had another experience that wasn't on my map of possibilities. This evening's tape was a lecture I'd been waiting for, Maharishi explaining the mechanics of creation.

"Being becomes conscious of itself and thereby becomes consciousness, eh? And from this—" he paused dramatically, eyebrows raised "—comes space. He held up one square hand on one side to illustrate.

"When being knows itself to be existing, there is a knower and—" he held up the other hand some distance from the other one "—a known. Between them there is space. But these two are not separate from each other. They are the same thing.

"Being—" he raised a finger on one hand "—and Consciousness—" then a finger on the other hand. "Being is conscious of its own existence. Knower and known. Eh?" He made a questioning sound and looked around to see if his audience was with him.

"And between these two aspects of the absolute, waves spring up. Waves, harmonics of waves, harmonics of harmonics. And this is creation." He paused again.

Everyone in the lecture hall was quiet, listening intently to the video, writing in notebooks and on pads propped on laps. I loved these abstract, esoteric tapes, at least that's how I experienced them at the time.

On the tape, Maharishi smiled and picked up a chrysanthemum. His hair fell in soft folds down onto his white robe. He toyed with the string of red coral beads hanging around his neck which often got wrapped up in his flowers. Red coral beads were all the rage among meditators.

"The nature of these waves is bliss, *ananda*. When Being becomes aware of itself, waves of joy spring up. Therefore—" another dramatic pause to indicate he was going to make an important point "—the basic nature of all creation is bliss."

I felt a glow start inside, as if a butterscotch sun had melted in my chest, leaving a pool of melted gold. *This is what I came here to learn*, I thought.

The glow deepened and pulled at me, reaching up to draw me in. I went with it, closing my eyes, floating down into the golden light inside. *This must be from meditating so much* was the last thought I had.

I floated inside the golden pool of completeness, content. The color began to change, ripple, then cleared. Maharishi's face appeared. I knew it was really him, not just a picture in my head. I bowed my head, my whole being waiting.

What's this about you and your friend? He thought to me, the sound gentle and lilting up. The question contained the knowledge of the whole situation. All our feelings were understood.

I love her, I sent back without speaking.

He returned a surge of understanding, unflinching, like a nod. It felt like *of course.* There was no question about me loving a woman.

He thought to me, *If you love her, then you will do as I ask.*

I hesitated only a second. Although he had not said it, I knew he was asking us not to see each other. He was saying *if you love her, you will let go of her and allow this lesson to unfold. Love means promoting the loved one's spiritual growth as the highest goal, even if that means leaving, even for a lifetime.* A lifetime was nothing in this place where Maharishi and I had met. There must be a lesson for us in this situation.

I will do whatever you ask of me.

He nodded and then opened the thin gate that had separated us, allowing the conversation. We flowed together, master and disciple, ocean and river, and there was no distinction between us for a moment.

Perhaps this could qualify as another samadhi experience, but I don't remember it that way. Minutes later, I began to hear Maharishi's voice from the TV monitor again. I sat in this total peace for a little longer, to remember it. Then I opened my eyes. Beth was looking at me curiously, her attention like heat pressing on me.

I moved away. The implications of this experience were now beginning to rise in my mind. I'd just agreed to leave Beth, for however long it took. Whatever 'it' was. Maybe this is why I've never thought of this as a flash of enlightenment. Too much pain and confusion followed on its heels. But sometimes, that's the way these things work.

I looked around the room. Everything was the same—the tape was still playing, everyone was listening, taking notes contently. Melinda and Jack Trapp were sitting on the dais on either side of the photo of Guru Dev.

Guru Dev, Swami Brahmananda Saraswati, Shankaracharya of Jyotir Mat
Photo by Theresa Crater

I remembered the tapes about release of stress during retreats, how extra meditations increased the body's purification to such a rate that stress release happened all the time—during sleep, dreams, meditation, and activity. That was the reason people were told not to make any major decisions or go beyond the course facilities alone. Maharishi said that people had strong moods during retreats, and vivid images during meditation that seemed real, and that these were all the result of purification. That they should be glad the stress was gone and not pay any attention to the content of the thoughts or moods.

I decided what I had just experienced was stress release, although I knew that this conversation had been as real as the chair I was sitting on. The course pooh-poohed the possibility of cosmic experiences in people just becoming teachers. After all, I was doing six meditations a day and under a lot of pressure. Why should I have had this advanced experience when I'd been told repeatedly that Maharishi considered it impossible? It must have been illusory, just my mind playing tricks on me. I hadn't just experienced union with the master.

In truth, the tension between the two impossible things was too great for me to manage. I firmly pushed this explanation to the fore—this experience had not been real; It had been stress release—and I forgot the agreement I just made.

But Maharishi remembered.

During the next Friday morning meeting, I noticed Daniel come into the lecture hall and sit in the back for a while. He had the answer for us about whether or not we could stay together. I looked to see if Beth had noticed him, but she was busy writing, her notebook propped on her leg, ankle crossed over her knee. I reached over and wrote on the top of Beth's page, *Daniel's here.*

Beth glanced around the room, then wrote under my note, *I guess we'll know soon.*

After the tape, I tried to find him, but he'd disappeared. We went to lunch but neither of us could eat. Beth sat staring outside at the thin flakes of snow that were starting to fall, taking an occasional bite. I pushed shepherd's pie and salad around on my plate for a while, then went to get dessert, raspberry cobbler cooked in huge, rectangular pans. Waiting in line, I saw Daniel walking out of the course leaders' private dining room. I headed after him. I called his name as he rounded the corner and headed up the wide stone stairway.

He turned and saw me, hesitated, then walked toward me with his customary wide smile. "Theresa, hello."

I started to speak, but he continued. "I do have a personal message for you from Maharishi, and I want to find the right time to talk with you and Beth privately. Say tonight, after the meeting? Good," he said without waiting for a reply. "Let's meet in the manager's office after the tape."

"Couldn't we talk with you any sooner? The waiting has been a little hard."

"I can imagine it has, but I have a lot of business to attend to, and my time is spoken for until tonight. I really appreciate your patience." He turned and headed up the stairs without a backward glance.

"But—" I reached out toward the stairs Daniel was climbing, suddenly filled with a high pitch panic, feeling like my skin was stretched too tight over the china bones of my face. My hand fell to my side. The other still held the bowl I'd carried for cobbler.

I walked back into the dining room and over to the dessert table. I stared down at two forks lying in a small puddle of raspberry juice. There weren't even any berries left. "Shit," I muttered, a small tear creeping out the corner of my eye.

"Don't take it so hard." I turned to see a man in a blue corduroy suit with gold wire rims. "It was just pie."

Finally, we were sitting in the manager's office with Daniel and maybe the last person had interrupted us. I couldn't believe the things people insisted on talking to Daniel about. And he just talked to them. He didn't tell them to wait as he told me. One person had wanted to know if it was all right to fast even though Maharishi had expressly forbidden it during this course. Another wanted to know if they were going to be able to meditate more. Someone complained about his room. Somebody else was waiting to hear from a friend in Switzerland.

"This suspense is really getting to be fun, don't you think?" Daniel said with a twinkle in his eye.

Beth just stared at him, dumbfounded.

When one more woman walked up and asked if she could interrupt just for a minute, I shouted "No!" but the woman stood outside the door listening instead of going away.

Daniel told her twice he would be a while and would talk to her in the morning, but she just kept standing there. When I opened my mouth to tell the woman off, Daniel jumped up, took the woman by the elbow, and walked her away from the door. He was back in two minutes and closed the door firmly behind him.

"Well," he said as he settled himself cozily into the high-backed chair behind the desk that belonged to the resort manager, "I did get an opportunity to speak with

Maharishi about your circumstances."

Someone knocked on the door, but he didn't move to open it. He smiled mischievously. "Are you sure you want to hear this tonight? Mother Nature certainly is giving us a hard time here. Maybe we should wait until tomorrow morning." Then he laughed.

I laughed too, by now punchy and slightly hysterical from the tension and delay. "Sure, why not?"

We both laughed.

Beth glowered at us. "For Christ's sake, would you just tell us?" she said, leaning forward in her chair.

Daniel and I burst out laughing again.

"What's the matter with you?" Beth demanded, glaring at me.

Daniel made an effort to compose himself, deliberately not looking at me. "Well, of course you're concerned and want to hear right away." He straightened himself in the chair, clearing his throat, then smiled again. "But remember, we're working for infinite flexibility here. That means equanimity in the face of any and all circumstances," he mildly chastised Beth.

"Equanimity is a product of cosmic consciousness, not the path to it, or have you forgotten that?" Beth snapped.

"Yes, well," Daniel temporized. "Actually, I waited to talk to you because I was . . . confused by Maharishi's message. And, frankly, I was surprised to see you two still together when I arrived." He sat and looked at us, letting this sink in.

We stared at each other, then I leaned forward. "What are you talking about?"

Daniel sat for a minute, tapping his finger on his chin. Then he said, "I can only tell you what Maharishi said. It took me a few days to get in to see him. When I did, of course, I had several questions for him. When I came to your situation, he said something odd."

"What?" Beth asked.

"He asked me your names, the course you were on, and then listened to the details. When I asked if you two could speak with him personally about the situation, he said he'd already spoken with you."

I inhaled sharply, remembering the conversation we'd had in my mind, the one I'd dismissed based on the movement's teachings. At the time I didn't realize this was basically gaslighting, teaching people to trust an organization rather than their own experience. But here my conversation with Maharishi was being confirmed.

Daniel looked at me expectantly. "He said the matter was already settled, that you'd agreed to separate."

Beth looked back and forth between us. "We never agreed to separate. That's ridiculous."

"When did you talk to him?" I asked in a quiet voice.

"Let me see," Daniel closed his eyes, thinking.

"This is ridiculous. We haven't talked to Maharishi," Beth repeated.

"When?" I asked, ignoring Beth.

Daniel sat back in his chair. "I got back to International Headquarters on

Saturday, but I didn't get in to talk to Maharishi until late on Monday evening."

"Oh my God."

Beth stared at me. "What's going on?" she finally asked. "You mean you called him? Why didn't you tell me?"

"Yes," Daniel said in a quiet, gentle voice. "What's going on? Do you understand what Maharishi meant?"

Beth protested weakly. "He hasn't talked to us. How could she understand what he meant?"

Daniel ignored her.

I looked up at Beth, an expression of deep regret in her eyes. "I'm sorry."

"Sorry? What are you talking about?" Beth's laugh was a little too loud.

I reached out toward Beth, then dropped my hands in my lap. Looking down at them, I started to speak. "I did talk to Maharishi. At least I think I did. But, when it happened, I didn't realize that it had been real." I looked up at Daniel again. "What time did you talk to him on Monday?"

Daniel thought for a moment. "Probably around ten that night, maybe later."

"But this happened earlier. How could he have known?"

"Time is a funny thing. I've given up trying to figure out how Maharishi knows what he knows." He smiled gently. "Why don't you tell us what happened?"

"What are you talking about?" Beth shouted.

I looked at her. "He came to me and asked what the problem was. When I explained—"

"Wait a minute," Beth interrupted. "What do you mean 'he came to you'?"

"Remember the night I told you I felt like I'd talked to Maharishi?"

"But you said you were just unstressing," Beth said.

"Yes, I know. I didn't understand how it could have happened, but I knew it was real. I just didn't want to admit it to myself."

"Admit what?" Daniel asked.

I looked at him, then at Beth. "Maharishi asked me to separate from you. And I agreed." Tears filled my eyes.

Beth stared at me in silence for a long minute, her mouth opening and closing like a fish. Daniel sat silent. Then she asked, "Why would you—why would he—?" Her voice was shrill, on the verge of hysteria. "What are you talking about?"

"I don't know how to explain it to you. I didn't realize what I was doing," I
said between sobs. "No, I realized it, it just didn't—oh, how can I make you understand?" I put my head in my hands and tried to catch my breath.

"Why don't you just explain things exactly as they happened?" Daniel suggested quietly.

I took a shaky breath and told them about my experience.

Beth stared at me uncomprehendingly.

I shook my head. "I just don't know how to tell you what it felt like. It's not only that I talked to him, Beth." I put my hand on the arm of Beth's chair in an appeal. "It's that by talking to him, mind to mind like that, I . . . there's no other way to explain it. I became one with him. I saw things from his perspective."

Beth pulled away sharply.

"It's not because we are lovers. Maharishi seemed to accept our relationship. It's something else," I said, my voice begging Beth to listen. "It's a question of our evolution."

Beth groaned her protest.

"Honestly. That might sound ridiculous to you, but nothing is more important than that, not even our being together. He said *if you love her, you will do as I ask.* He's interested in our welfare." I was finally silent.

Beth brushed blindly at a tear that rolled down her cheek.

"Well," Daniel said after a long pause. "Now I understand Maharishi's message. What do you intend to do, Theresa?"

I looked at Daniel, then at Beth, who stared back.

"How could you do this to me?" Beth whispered.

"I wish I could make you understand."

"I'll never understand and I don't agree to separate," she said.

"I asked Maharishi what to do in case one of you said this, and his answer was that he would see you both in Switzerland on your way home from leaving this course. These are the only circumstances under which he will see you if you agree to leave the teacher's course."

"I won't leave. I agree to separate," I said, avoiding Beth's eyes.

"No!" she shouted.

I stared at the floor.

Beth stood, a grizzly in a cage. "I refuse to separate," she shouted. "I'm going to see Maharishi. If you want to really talk to him, come with me. Otherwise, stay here with your friends." She turned and walked out of the room.

I sat in stunned silence. Daniel remained sitting quietly behind the manager's desk. I stared at the doorway and listened to the silence left in the wake of Beth's departure. The whole hotel seemed to be asleep. Outside the snow fell whisper quiet, making tiny wet plashes against the windowpane. I was deeply calm and as cold as the snow outside. After what seemed like a long time, I looked up at Daniel but couldn't think of anything to say. I looked around the room at the green metal file cabinet, the old chairs, the faded mountain scene framed on the wall, then back at Daniel. I smiled weakly. "I guess I can't sit here all night."

Daniel smiled back, a warm light in his eyes. "You know," he said quietly, "when we start meditating, we think we're just adding twenty minutes twice a day to our lives, and for some this seems like a big sacrifice." He leaned back in the chair. "Little can we imagine what changes will come. Your course hasn't studied puja yet, but this reminds me of the opening lines. 'Whether pure or impure, whoever opens himself to unbounded awareness gains inner and outer purity.' When we start to meditate we cannot imagine the ramifications." He spread his hands in front of him. "Maybe it's a good thing."

"I wouldn't exactly describe myself as impure," I said stiffly.

Daniel chuckled. "I didn't mean offense. To me, serving with Maharishi every day, and seeing him regularly, we are all very far from purity. But your heart is pure, Theresa. Your heart is as pure as that snow outside, and I think you have what it takes to make it."

"I don't want to hurt Beth. I never meant for this to happen."

"As I said, your heart is pure. But you will hurt her, and yourself, if you don't do what you know is right." He leaned forward and looked at me intently. "Neither you nor I know why nature is demanding this of you. I can't say that your relationship with Beth is wrong. It's not up to me to make that judgment. But nature has demanded that you make this sacrifice now, and you have accepted it. You have surrendered to the will of Mother Nature. The pain will pass. Nature will support you now that you've made the right decision."

"But I'm...." I closed my eyes against the tears, "scared. I don't know what to do next. This wasn't in the plan. It's like stepping off a cliff."

"When Govinda saw his master in the middle of the river and the coming flood, he didn't have a boat and he couldn't swim. But he didn't stop to consider this. He just walked into the flood. And everywhere he stepped, a lotus blossom grew to support his foot. Just step out. You've made the decision nature demands of you. She will support you, every step of the way."

3

I CAN'T REALLY SAY THAT this separation was what Mother Nature wanted from me or if Maharishi was right in asking for it. Perhaps this was all just prejudice against LGBTQ people, although that acronym didn't even exist then. LGBT was first used in 1988. It has accumulated a few more letters since then.

Beth and I were good together in many ways. We would have made a strong teaching team, but our relationship didn't survive all of this. I hardly saw her after we went to separate courses. We were in the same town, but in different accommodations and lecture halls.

The medical team operated out of the new hotel I was moved to. She came by occasionally, more to see me than to get any treatments. I remember once being summoned into one of the treatment rooms and there she lay, acupuncture needles quivering as she tried to turn her head and look at me while we talked.

My father died within a week of us returning from the course and funeral arrangements and grief overwhelmed me. I didn't think much about teacher training for a while. Beth stood by me, but distance had crept into our relationship and soon it won out. When we applied to the next part of the teacher training course, we got more resistance. Beth was forced to move away to another area to work for a center and get a so-called "objective evaluation." Beth and I lost track of each other for a long time.

Meanwhile, I stayed at my local TM center and applied for the next phase of the teacher training course. Why? The TM technique had already revealed to me areas of consciousness and experiences that I'd never imagined were possible. The movement taught they held the only way forward. I was young. I was naïve enough to believe them. I wanted enlightenment more than anything else.

So, I stayed.

Gay and lesbian people were discriminated against everywhere. People were fired if their employer discovered their sexuality. They were thrown out of their apartment. Churches and synagogues and their own families rejected them. And here I'm saying *them*. I was also not safe anywhere. Not really.

I found an unexpected ally. The local center had a new teacher who I'll call Holly. She was disgusted with the way Beth and I had been treated at our first teacher training course. Privately, she asked why we'd ever told the local center that we were lesbians. She was from the north, had worked in a large corporation. She had more worldly experience that I did.

We'd had similar questions from a few gay people on our course in Livigno. One older man told us about some rather harrowing experiences in the 1950s, how bars were raided, people beaten up on the streets. Of course, this happens today, but then it was simply the risk gay men and lesbians took. It was the way things were. Just life. Law enforcement did nothing to stop it. He said he knew better than to trust straight people knowing about him, especially people in the movement.

Holly planned to go off to a new and advanced six-month course that was scheduled at the same time as the next phase of teacher training. Everyone was all abuzz about the new teachings Maharishi was bringing out. What would they be? The flyer that was sent around said he wanted his most advanced meditators to gather and "experiment with consciousness as a field of all possibilities by exploring ancient Vedic techniques hand-in-hand with modern scientific discoveries in physics and chemistry."

I had received full endorsement from the center for the second half of the teacher training course and was waiting for my final acceptance to go through. The time for the charter flight crept closer with no word. I started to get nervous, but Holly took things into her own hands. She called the national organization, insisting on hearing from international staff.

Her boldness amazed me. I was the child of a father who worked in a factory and a mother who sold shoes in a high-end retail store. I'd been taught to be obedient. Holly knew her way around the world. Beth had amazed me, too, when a leak in our rented apartment ruined her good coat. After a lot of back and forth, the landlord reimbursed her and reduced our rent for one month. I was amazed. I hadn't realized how obedient my upbringing had taught me to be, even after marching in civil rights and anti-war protests.

The national office said I'd been given special instructions by Jack and Melinda Trapp and hadn't followed them, so I had to fulfill these conditions before going forward. Yes, the Trapps raised their ugly heads again. I'd never received any instructions from them. They lied. I was still capable of being shocked by that. My new advocate pressed and argued—nicely, of course, because showing anger was a sure sign of "unstressing" and instability. At least according to the movement. But the day of our charter flight to Europe arrived and I still hadn't gotten accepted.

"Just come to Europe anyway," Holly said. "I'll help you get a position on staff. Then you can get close to Maharishi directly and ask his permission to go to the course."

I was beyond amazed. I was shocked by the idea. But I did it anyway. This is how I ended up asking Maharishi in person if I could go to teacher training, but not before enduring more harassment from international staff.

I was assigned a job working in the hotel where Holly's course was happening. The course was large and the women had three hotels. I don't even remember where the men were lodged. In the next few weeks, I got to know most of the women in the small hotel, but especially Holly's new gang—Elena, Nicole, and Tina (not their real names). I ate dinner with them after I served the food, walked with them when I could, and hung out in Holly's room on Thursdays, the day of rest in India, and sometimes after evening meetings to talk.

Elena, who'd been on international staff and was the most politically savvy when it came to the movement, sent me on gossip-foraging trips to the Annapurna Hotel where Maharishi was living. The staff orbited around him. I never returned with anything very startling. I suspected it was because I wore kitchen clothes and international staff people were circumspect when they saw me. I could have worn a dress, but I often didn't have the time to change. I enjoyed simply walking around in the subdued bustle of the nerve center of Maharishi's international organization.

Holly and the gang were closed-mouthed with me about what the series of initiations had brought them. They took hours and hours in their rooms doing what Holly was now calling "the program," and they were more forgetful as the days progressed. I began to feel a bit cut off, but I set that aside. It was to be expected and, besides, everyone supported my desire to speak with Maharishi privately. Holly had told them my way to the teacher's course was being blocked by former course leaders who had told a lie about me.

The gang schemed up ways for me to see Maharishi, and once I managed to walk into the hotel with him and explain my predicament, in front of at least 100 people. Not at all intimidating. He had asked me when the next teacher's course was beginning and told me to come speak with him one week before it began. I had three weeks to wait.

The whole incident was a blur. At the time, I viewed Maharishi as an enlightened being, my spiritual master, full of wisdom and knowledge, someone who was beyond common human mistakes because of his connection to the universal mind.

One day while I was sitting at dinner with the gang, Holly's course leader walked up to the table and told Holly she wanted to see her before the lecture. After a second helping of Stefan's rhubarb pie, Holly walked off to find her. Just as they walked into the lecture hall together, I noticed the man in charge of the hotel staff walk in the front door. When he spotted me and gestured for me to join him, I took my dishes to the kitchen, then followed him to two chairs in the vestibule of the hotel, a dull knot forming in my stomach.

He smiled. "Have a seat."

I sat, knees pressed tightly together.

He cleared his throat. " I've just come from the advanced course administrators. They are concerned about your friendship with the women in this hotel."

I took a sharp breath, but he pressed on. "They feel that, given your past history, it is inappropriate for you to be working here."

"What?"

"I asked them where they felt you could work, and they said that, after talking with the teacher's course office, they felt it was inappropriate for you to be here at all. So, they have authorized me to pay your way back to the States. A charter is leaving in two days—"

"Just wait a minute," I said, feeling a dizzying *déjà vu*. "Why can't I work here?"

"Because you haven't fulfilled your special instructions."

"There never were any special instructions," I said, my voice rising.

He looked at me sadly. "The Trapps have been very explicit about this. And there have been reports about your relationship with Holly."

"Relationship? I'm celibate. Holly and I come from the same center. We're friends."

The staff representative's face was a mask.

I puffed out my frustration and sat back heavily in the chair. "Great, so now

I can't have any friends." I didn't realize at the time how childish this sounded.

Then, a way out occurred to me. "I need to speak with Maharishi before I leave."

"I'm afraid that will be impossible. Maharishi is not available."

"I must speak with him. He told me to see him next week. I can't leave without speaking with him."

"Maharishi is in the States. He is unavailable. You are not eligible to work on International Staff. You must leave. Tomorrow." He stood and looked down at his shoes. "Be ready with your bags in the lobby in the morning. We will take you to meet the charter."

Before I could protest, he turned and left.

I looked wildly around the lobby. The course participants were filing into their lecture hall. Holly was nowhere to be seen. I walked into the dining room. No Holly. I looked in the door and saw her standing in a tight knot with Elena and Tina. I waved to get her attention. Holly looked up, saw me, and frowned. I waved more emphatically.

The course leader spotted me and headed toward me. Elena turned and interrupted her approach by asking her a question. Tina slipped out of the lecture hall. "Holly says she can't talk to you right now, but that she knows what's happened. They're threatening Holly, too."

"Oh, no. Who's been talking to them?"

"We don't know, but we're going to find out. Nicole's going to pull some strings. There's no way we'll let this happen to Holly. And we hope we can just get you transferred, not sent home. Then you can still try to see Maharishi. Meanwhile, you should go pack. One thing is certain. You won't be able to stay in this hotel. And don't try to see Holly right now. She's freaked."

Tina looked into my eyes. "Don't worry, sweetie. We won't let them send you home. You'll become a teacher in spite of this."

Nicole definitely pulled some strings. I moved to a new hotel, an ancient hunting lodge, where I was the receptionist for another section of the advanced course. All day long I stared at the huge elk head mounted on the wall as if it were an oracle that would one day burst into speech and give me a prophecy that would explain all this. I'd been here for a week and a half, in Europe for over a month now. In addition to sorting mail and answering phones, I made juice for the women who were fasting, a tedious job. They complained about everything, but I ignored them, knowing as only the shell-shocked could that they didn't have anything to complain about.

I managed to see Holly only once for twenty minutes, and it had been an uncomfortable meeting, with Holly constantly looking over her shoulder as we talked in a dark corner of her hotel basement. She said the gang thought they'd figured out who'd snitched on them, and she was busy trying to mend fences and convince everyone that she had not known of my past.

"Gee, thanks," I said.

"Well, what do you expect?"

"I don't know. I just wish you weren't so eager to separate yourself from me."

"My friends are still supporting you. I'm doing what I need to survive. This is very stressful for me."

"I'm sorry. I appreciate what you and the others have done, really."

"Just sit tight. When Maharishi comes to our hotel, we'll send for you. We have to be very careful. Don't let anyone see you leave. I have to go back to my room now."

"Goodbye."

"And don't talk in your new hotel."

"Talk? Who am I—" but Holly had already turned and soon disappeared into the black of the basement.

So, I was waiting for the chance to see Maharishi and straighten this mess out. The women in the hotel where I was working had been expecting him for days, but I knew not to count on rumor. One night I was carrying a huge pan of au gratin potatoes up the ancient stone stairs. I'd come down to eat and been recruited to help in the kitchen at the last minute. I reached the landing where the elk's head hung and paused to get a better grip on the pan I was carrying. The woman who was in charge of the course came running out of the dining room toward me. "Uwe is looking for you." (I don't remember his real name.)

"Who?"

She shook her head impatiently and gestured for me to hurry. "He's in here."

I walked into the dining room toward the serving table, but the woman pointed to the one man in the room who was standing apart from everyone, a long, white apron still tied around his waist, tall rubber boots on his feet. He was holding a wool hat in his hands. I recognized Uwe, the cook from Holly's hotel.

He blinked. "Theresa?"

"Yes."

"They told me to come to get you. Maharishi wants to see you now."

At last.

I turned, gave the pan of potatoes to the woman still standing beside me, and started for my coat. Then I turned back and looked at her. "What should I wear?"

She laughed and said, "Your best, of course, but you mustn't keep Maharishi waiting, so go as you are."

I looked down and remembered I had put on my best brown dress to come down to dinner and was relieved. Some part of me must have known this was going to happen. At least that's what I thought at the time.

"I need to put on my boots," I said to Uwe.

"Yes, but I think boots are not very good for seeing Maharishi," he said, shaking his head. His previous arrogant attitude toward me had evaporated.

"We have to climb over the hill in the snow," I called over my shoulder.

I ran to my room, grabbed my coat, and laced up my tooled leather boots as quickly as I could, skipping a few grommets, then raced back to the dining room. We left the hotel, Uwe leading the way. The knee-deep snowbanks forced us to slow motion. I tried to capture the deep silence of the stars shining bright in the sky as I struggled toward this goal I'd worked for during the last two months.

When I walked through the door of Holly's hotel, Tina ushered me to a chair in the lobby and helped me out of my coat. She pointed for me to take off her boots, then whispered, "We saw a chance for you to get in to see Maharishi, so we sent for you.

Elena's with him now. You can go in after her."

A small clump of women stood near the door of the lecture hall. Holly was standing by the door behind Nicole, who was squared off with a woman I recognized from the Annapurna.

"Maharishi is here to speak with members of this course," the staff woman said. "If Theresa wants to speak with him, she can make an appointment through his personal secretary."

Nicole said, "He's here right now and he told her a few weeks ago to come and talk to him when the next part of teacher training was starting." She was speaking slowly and carefully as if she was explaining some natural phenomenon to a child. "A new course is starting next week. Now is the ideal time for her to speak with him. We don't mind giving up five minutes of our time with Maharishi to her."

Holly spotted me and gestured for me to join her by the door. But the staff woman saw me and started toward me. Tina blocked her way. "Maharishi himself told Theresa not to seek him out at the Annapurna, but to see him when he came back to the hotel," Tina said.

Holly took me behind the group of women at the door and whispered intently, "Elena just went in."

We could see her sitting in front of Maharishi, her long, blond hair a braid down her back. She looked prim and proper, like a young woman at confirmation. I smoothed my dress with nervous hands. Why were these women putting themselves on the line for me?

"This matter is being handled by the teacher's course office—" the staff woman began.

"'*Handled*' is right," Nicole interrupted. "Don't pretend to us that you will arrange for Theresa to see Maharishi because I know that you'll just try to stop her. It used to be that he was available to everyone."

Maharishi glanced back at the cluster of women at the doorway with a frown. A chorus of shushes followed. Nicole lowered her voice. "Now International Staff decides who can talk to him and who can't. Even if he's asked to see them."

The woman drew herself up to her full height. I turned back to watch Elena's back intently, an ear cocked to this conversation. "No one on staff ever interferes with

Maharishi's wishes. We are here to serve him. We carry out his requests."

Tina spoke in soothing tones. "I'm sure that the staff tries to serve Maharishi to the letter of his word but you were, unfortunately, not in the hotel to hear exactly what he said to her last month, and we were. We are also doing what he requested by bringing her here today."

"Theresa." It was the staff woman's voice.

"Ignore her," Holly whispered.

"You can't go in to see Maharishi today. He only set aside one hour to be here and there are two more ladies who wish to speak with him. Then he must talk with the whole course."

My eyes flickered to the staff woman's face.

"Surely you respect Maharishi's time more than this. He has chosen to speak to the advanced ladies tonight. You will be acting against his wishes if you go in there, and the teacher's course staff must be notified of your attitude."

"I'm supposed to go in next and she can have my turn," Tina said firmly.

The staff woman refused to acknowledge Tina, trying to hold my eyes.

"Elena's getting up," Holly whispered in my ear.

I looked into the room. Elena was standing. She paused a moment, then took a flower Maharishi handed to her.

"Theresa, you can't go in there," the staff woman said.

Holly put a flower in my hand and stood behind me, hands on my shoulders. I wondered how I would explain myself to Maharishi. I remembered our mental conversation during the evening lecture at the last teacher training course, his easy acceptance of my love for Beth.

"Go in, Theresa," Nicole said.

"Go on," Tina said.

"You can't go in," the staff woman said firmly.

"Go on," Nicole said.

"She can't go in," the staff woman repeated.

Elena turned and walked toward the door.

"Now," Holly said and shoved me into the room.

"No," the staff woman said, reaching out for my arm.

Maharishi's head lifted at the sound. He smiled and gestured for me to come forward. The staff woman fell back, acquiescing.

My brain was numb. It had all happened so quickly that I had no internal motivation yet. I walked mechanically down the aisle, propelled solely by Holly's push, then plopped the orange flower Holly had given me into Maharishi's small, squared-off palm without glancing at him.

"Jai Guru Dev," I muttered and sat abruptly in the chair that had been pulled up to face his couch on the dais.

Maharishi frowned slightly, visibly surprised by my approach, then a mischievous smile played around the corners of his mouth, and he sat waiting for me to begin.

I immediately felt ridiculous and pulled at my dress to cover my knees. I had to say something. I looked up. His face was the picture of serious attention, but his eyes danced, amused.

He isn't going to take me seriously, I thought.

"Maharishi."

"Eh?" He gave one of his inquiring and encouraging little sounds and raised the eyebrows above his dancing eyes.

I was startled by the familiarity of this sound, heard hundreds of times through tape recorders and television speakers. The same sound. It reassured me somehow. "I spoke with you last month about going to Part Two of the teacher's course. You see," I took a breath.

I'd gone over this a hundred times with Holly, what to say. I wanted to ask him if it was okay, after all, my love for a woman, but sitting here in front of him, I couldn't speak the words. I couldn't talk about sex in this room with flowers and white everywhere, even if it had seemed holy under the stars. I couldn't talk about loving a woman with this monk who was looking deep into my soul and seemed to know what I was thinking before I did.

He was waiting. I took the safe road.

"I was involved in a, uh, non-life-supporting relationship . . ."

By this time I'd rationalized that my relationship with Beth had stopped being good for each of us long before it had ended. I'd talked about it with Holly many times, how it had been nature's way of ending that relationship and setting us both on our paths again. Now, I don't think this at all. It's amazing the things we will tell ourselves to keep from losing something we attach ourselves to so deeply.

". . . but that's all over with now and I want to go on to the teacher's course. The course office won't let me." I stopped.

Maharishi laughed.

He's laughing at me, I thought. I took a breath to protest, but no words came.

"You must let your national leaders handle this. Write a letter and explain." It was so simple to him. In his world the sun was always shining and everyone wanted to do the right thing. That's what I imagined at the time.

"But there's no time. The course starts in three days."

Maharishi laughed again, leaning back against the cushions, delighted. He waved his flower in the air to dismiss my objection because what I'd said was true. There is no time. Time does not exist. That was his reality.

"Just write." He waved his hand. "One or two letters will clear up the entire misunderstanding."

That was his final answer, I could tell. His eyes strayed to the door. I could argue with him, try to persuade him to change his mind, simply ask to be sent on to the course around this hurdle he'd placed in my way.

But then this thought rose. *I came here to ask my master a question and now I have his answer. Am I disciple enough to accept it or am I going to sit here and argue with him, try to bend him to my will when I should bend to his?*

I sat back in the chair. I would do as he asked. I would write to national, even though I knew it would do no good. I would step off the next cliff just because Maharishi had asked me to. I accepted my fate.

Sitting there empty, a thought came. *Maharishi's eyes. I've always wanted just to look into them.*

I raised my head. Maharishi was looking down at me, waiting. His eyes twinkled.

When our eyes met, we connected somehow. He was a deep pool of vibrant energy, unlimited. He laughed, delighted that I had found him. His laughter rippled out from the pool and touched me.

The touch woke me up. I saw that I was the same as Maharishi. I was infinite, too. I was, in fact, Maharishi exactly. And I felt the ripple that was both Maharishi and I extend out of the room, across the mountains, and into the night sky. Everything was the same. One unlimited consciousness.

We looked into each other's eyes and burst out laughing. We laughed long and full at the delightful joke of it all. About how one piece of infinity came to another piece of infinity asking to be made infinite. Asking in desperation, out of a crying need, in deep pain. And the joke was not only that this piece of infinity wanting so desperately to be infinite already was. But that I could not even have been searching, could not have even conceived infinity if I hadn't already been exactly what I was looking for.

We laughed for what seemed like a long time.

It was as if I'd been born in a house and all my life heard stories of a great mansion where a person could have anything she wanted, things she could never have even conceived of. And she'd grown desperate to find this place, running from room to room asking everyone if they knew how to find this mansion. Finally, she'd knocked on the last door and found the last person in the house, and she'd said, "Tell me, where is this great mansion? Tell me or I'll die."

And he had said, "This is it."

She'd never known this was the place she had searched for because she had never even been away from it. You can't find what you haven't lost.

I looked at Maharishi now and it didn't matter if I went to this teacher's course I had come to ask him about. In fact, it didn't matter if I ever went. In this lifetime or in three. Nothing mattered because there was no lack in the universe.

A faint whisper went through my mind. *You will forget this.*

I knew that when I left his presence my experience would fade and I would begin to search again. I thought about asking Maharishi what to do when this happened, but I knew that even that didn't matter because I could never truly be lost. Even the search was a part of the whole.

I simply stood and we said in unison, "Jai Guru Dev." And meant it.

Maharishi pulled off a purple bud from the long gladiola stem he held and I accepted it. We laughed one more time and then I turned and walked out of the hall.

4

SO THAT'S THE WHOLE STORY. Why did sitting with Maharishi uplift me into this spontaneous experience of enlightenment and how did it change me? Was Maharishi a fully enlightened being? I can't say. What was the trigger that opened me up? Did he reach out and grant me *darshan* or give me *shaktipat*, the transmission of spiritual energy from one person to another?

Maybe just sitting with Maharishi tuned me to a higher frequency. This happens with musical instruments. Take two violins, for example. Put them next to each other. Strike a note on one several times in a row. This sets up a vibration that will transfer to the other one. The second violin will start to emit the same note. Humans vibrate, too. In fact, physics tells us everything is simply vibrating energy. How solid we are is determined by how slow or rapid the vibration is. This was certainly happening during my interview with him. This happens all the time, in fact. Ever go into a room and feel your mood drop or elevate? This has something to do with the frequency of the place.

I think the key lies elsewhere, though. I was wondering about this the other day and got a hint from Krishna Das. My husband and I – yes, I'm with a man now. I've always been bisexual, but identified as a lesbian for more than twenty-five years. Would the TM movement be happy? Anyway, my husband and I often listen to Krishna Das on Thursday night when he does online satsang called "Hanging in the Heart Space." After chanting, he answers questions. Sometimes he tells a story that relates to a chant he's just done.

This night just after I'd been writing, he talked about a time when he couldn't chant with the people with whom he usually did satsang and concerts. He said that we probably knew the reason. I didn't know since I haven't closely followed the people who were taught by Neem Karoli Baba (Maharaj-Ji), his spiritual guru. I enjoy his talks, though, and was listening carefully.

Because he couldn't chant he went to the temple Maharaj-ji founded. The guru himself had left his body over twenty years before, but this didn't stop Krishna Das from asking him to intervene. Krishna Das was certain his guru could fix the situation, but his master didn't do anything. Krishna Das kept asking. He appealed to him for two months. Finally one night Krishna Das was standing behind the temple and he just accepted that his guru was not going to intervene. He was not going to fix the situation. Krishna Das knew he would have to fix it himself. He said he felt an inrush of uplifting energy when he made this decision.

What was the trigger, he asked? Surrender. He surrendered to the situation. He accepted it. He stopped struggling. This opened him up and when he fell silent, he experienced a rush of spiritual energy.

This is almost exactly what happened to me. I stopped struggling. I was no longer wrestling with my thoughts and emotions, trying to change the situation I was in. I just let go. And in letting go, I became available to the energy right in front of me. I bounced into Unity for a time.

A Buddhist would call this mindfulness. I opened to the present moment with no expectations. It's a bit like meditating. We start the practice and when we find ourselves drifting off in thoughts, we simply return our attention to our point of focus. As we do this day after day, year after year, our minds and bodies clear, and we are able to delve deeper and deeper into the stillness within.

I was correct that I would lose the luster of this moment when I woke up the next morning and went about my day. But I'd experienced Unity. I knew it was there. It was on my new map of possibilities.

I don't remember exactly how I made it to the teacher training course. It's written down somewhere. I wrote a novel about all this trying to figure out for myself how a group dedicated to bringing enlightenment to the world could be so, well, unenlightened. This will bring a chuckle to most advanced practitioners, people who've been meditating or chanting for decades. Ashrams, spiritual groups, are rife with ego and power struggles. All the human failures are on full display. But I was still a bit naïve when I wrote that novel. The experience of putting it all down, even in fictional form, helped purge my pain and sorrow.

I taught meditation for a while and still do from time to time, but I eventually left the movement. Many TM teachers did the same. Dogma seemed to overtake personal experience. The movement line was enforced above all else. People who questioned the party line were "unstressing" or "unevolved." This is my perception of things. I know many others who feel the same.

One of the things I learned from Maharishi that I've always valued was to verify any teaching through personal experience. Unity is an idea until we experience it. We might have good reason to believe in it, but until it is our own lived experience, it is just that. An idea. Coming home to one's own experience is an important part of any path. It keeps us balanced. It keeps us honest. But now I knew Unity Consciousness was a real possibility.

*** ✬✬✬

What is this heightened state of consciousness? How does one achieve it? Does it last or do we only just get glimpses? The Vedic teachings of enlightenment are given on the fourth night of each introductory TM course. They call it *a glimpse of possibilities*. What happens if we keep meditating regularly, the teacher asks? Yes, we sleep better, we're less stressed, and we begin to unfold our full potential, all the benefits that are talked about in the first introductory lecture. But what is our full potential? On this last night, new meditators learn about higher states of consciousness.

Maharishi taught that humans experience seven states of consciousness. Not all traditions teach the same number of states or even separate them so clearly as Maharishi did, but all spiritual traditions teach about enlightenment. This may come as a surprise to those of us raised in the Abrahamic religions—Judaism, Christianity, and Islam. Here the ideas are oblique and sometimes even hidden. I'll discuss this more about this later in this book.

What are these states of consciousness? The first three we're very familiar with and aren't much to write home about: waking, sleeping, and dreaming. Ideally, we cycle through them every twenty-four hours. Each of these states is different both objectively and subjectively. When I teach meditation, I explain that we could put a person in a separate room and hook them up to machines to read their brainwaves, oxygen levels, heart rate, blood pressure, etc. and tell what state of consciousness they're in based on the readings.

When we're awake, beta waves predominate in the brain. Doctors like our oxygen levels to be in the high nineties. Our heart rates vary according to our fitness level and if we're anxious or feeling calm, but the average resting heart rate is sixty to one hundred beats per minutes, with athletes averaging forty to fifty. Blood pressure is affected by our fitness and anxiety level as well, but again, there is a range that is considered normal.

Delta and theta waves dominate during sleep. Our respiration and heart rate slow. Telemetry can register theta waves during dreaming. We also experience rapid eye movement and our metabolism picks up a bit.

Subjectively, waking and dreaming have more in common than our experience during sleep. Sleep is mostly a blank for us, although this changes as we continue to meditate. Dreams take their imagery from our waking state for the most part, but what is possible there is quite different than what we experience in the collective reality of waking state, although scientists claim we experience subtle differences in the world. I asked my husband to hand me the purple plate from the cabinet the other day. He frowned and asked, "You mean the brown one?" and pointed to what I saw as purple.

The next four states are related more to meditation and progress toward developing our full potential. The transcendental state is usually achieved during meditation, although with some experience now, I can tell you the first time I transcended was listening to Bach as a teenager. Transcendental Consciousness occurs when the conscious mind settles down and merges with the One Consciousness underlying all life. It is a state of restful alertness. The mind is silent, but completely aware. As the founder of Zen, Wu Hsin, puts it, "Everyone is only a single thought away from perfection." He's quite the trickster, because the transcendent is awareness with no thought.

Physiologically, the transcendental state is different from sleep in that we experience even deeper rest. Our brain settles into alpha waves. As we continue to meditate and experience deeper states, theta waves predominate. Our heart rate drops significantly. We breathe much slower. Our blood pressure drops. During meditation, we get a deeper rest in twenty minutes than we do during sleep. Research has shown a seventeen percent drop in metabolism after twenty minutes of TM as opposed to a ten percent drop after sleep.[2]

---

[2] Chaya, M.S. and H.R. Nagendra. "Long-term effect of yogic practices on diurnal metabolic rates of healthy subjects." *International Journal of Yoga.* 2008 Jan-Jun; 1(1): 27-32.

In the early 1980s, I was in a new relationship with a naturopathic doctor, and during my meditation, she snuck into the room, put a cuff around my arm, and took my blood pressure. It was way low, even after all that kerfuffle. This convinced her there was some scientific data to back up what I had claimed about meditating.

When I was recovering from surgery, I woke up several times in the middle of the night, so I meditated to speed up my healing. Twice the nurse ran in to see what was happening to me because my heart rate and oxygen levels had dropped. Each time she'd ask me to take a deep breath and my oxygen levels would pop right back up. She told me what was happening and was not convinced that meditation was the cause. I've learned not to argue much with medical folks, but lately, they've started adding meditation, mindfulness, and yoga as treatment options. I call that progress!

The poet William Wordsworth expressed the experience of the transcendent beautifully:
...that blessed mood,
In which the burthen of the mystery,
In which the heavy and the weary weight
Of all this unintelligible world,
Is lightened:—that serene and blessed mood,
In which the affections gently lead us on,—
Until, the breath of this corporeal frame
And even the motion of our human blood
Almost suspended, we are laid asleep
In body, and become a living soul:
While with an eye made quiet by the power
Of harmony, and the deep power of joy,
We see into the life of things. (lines 42-50)[3]

---

[3] "Lines Composed a Few Miles above Tintern Abbey, On Revisiting the Banks of the Wye during a Tour." July 13, 1798. www.poetryfoundation.org. Accessed 13 August 2022.

This state doesn't usually last very long during meditation and is sometimes experienced as a blank, like sleep. This seems like a complete contradiction, right? But transcending happens in the blink of an eye. In the beginning, our nervous system isn't cultivated enough to stay merged or experience the transcendent very clearly. New meditators will say, "I know I wasn't asleep, but there was a blank." As we continue to meditate, this silent area of the mind becomes clearer. We experience this awareness more and more fully.

We even begin to maintain our connection while the mind becomes active again. Then even when we go back into activity in our daily lives. When we maintain our connection to the transcendent permanently, during waking, dreaming, and sleeping, we have entered the fifth state of consciousness. Maharishi called this Cosmic Consciousness, cosmic meaning all-encompassing. What's it like for our individual mind to be floating in the cosmic sea? The Vedic teaching is that we are in harmony with universal law. The structure of the universal mind is the structure of our mind. Our actions are in harmony with our highest purpose and with the unfoldment of all life.

We also experience what some people call witnessing. Our awareness, in harmony with One Consciousness, is still silent, watching activity as if it is separate. We look out at the world without being overwhelmed by it. There is a sense of detachment. One of my favorite lectures about moving from Cosmic Consciousness into the next state has to do with this detachment. I repeated this teaching with a male teacher at a weekend rounding course in the North Carolina mountains. He played the part of the intellect. I played the heart. A little gender stereotypical, but the TM movement is that way. If it wasn't, I wouldn't have needed to sit in front of Maharishi and beg to be allowed on the next teacher training course.

The intellect is satisfied with Cosmic Consciousness as the highest state. After all, the Absolute or One Consciousness is separate from its creation. All comes from it, but it remains there, watching everything grow and change and work its way back home. But is it really separate? The heart begins to feel restless in Cosmic Consciousness. Surely there is more, it feels. A yearning still remains. And when there is a tiny sense of lack, this means there is something to fill that lack.

As we continue to meditate and go about our daily activities in Cosmic Consciousness, our system continues to refine itself. Our senses become more subtle. We begin to perceive the subtler realms of manifestation. Our perceptions become celestial. "We see into the life of things," as Wordsworth wrote. When our senses become attuned to the subtlest realms of creation, we have reached a sixth state of consciousness. Maharishi called it God Consciousness. We become aware of the angelic realms, the home of the gods. Many of the special human abilities manifest themselves in this state—clairaudience, clairvoyance, knowing what others are thinking or feeling, communicating with animals and plants. These abilities lie in the subtle realms of the mind. Many people have these abilities well before full Cosmic Consciousness, but in God Consciousness we see their full flowering.

What could possibly come next? Just a slight shove and we arrive at Unity Consciousness. The divisions melt away. We see everything and everyone as Infinite. The Vedic expression for this progression from Cosmic Consciousness to God Consciousness and to Unity goes like this: "I am That, Thou art That, All this is That."

There are states even higher than Unity. The Vedas talk about Brahman Consciousness, the awareness that everything is only waves of energy moving through the immovable Absolute. That in fact there is no objective manifestation at all. The Persian poet Hafiz expressed it this way: "There are some who can visit that Luminous Sphere that reveals this life never was."[4] But, as Krishna Das might say, this is way above my pay grade.

---

[4] From *The Gift* translated by Daniel Ladinsky. There is some controversy that Ladinsky's translations are not close enough to the original. I am not a scholar in these matters and cannot speak to this, but it is worth noting.

The highest state in all the traditions is ascension into the light body. Yep, it's exactly what it sounds like. This is complete mastery of the physical plane. The person is able to transmute their body into light. They can then manifest a physical body whenever and wherever they wish. Some believe this is what Yeshua experienced and what is described in the Bible as the resurrection. Western metaphysics teaches that two ancient prophets achieved this state, one being Enoch. This prophet is said to have walked with God for three hundred years. Genesis 5:24 states "And Enoch walked with God: and he *was* not; for God took him." Second Kings tells us that Elijah was taken up in a fiery chariot. That just begs for a metaphysical interpretation, like kundalini maybe, but I can't say. All this is way beyond my pay grade.

Western metaphysics claims there is no end to this unfolding, that what we perceive as the One Consciousness is an entity who has manifested this universe, but is learning from the process and after finishing this, will 'graduate' to another level of awareness. Likewise, there are four levels to the Tree of Life, but each of those levels has four levels, and so on. It makes me dizzy.

As I mentioned earlier, the Abrahamic religions also speak of enlightenment, but most people raised in these traditions will tell you we are separate from God and it is therefore blasphemy to suggest we could merge with the Divine. The history of these faiths holds the key to why this has happened, something that would take a whole book to really unpack, and other people have written it. Briefly, the Council of Nicaea in 325 CE and subsequent ecumenical councils decided on the divinity of Jesus and which texts were to be included in the New Testament of the Bible. There is some dispute about this last bit, but Jerome (347-420 CE) in his Prologue to Judith makes the claim that the *Book of Judith* was approved by the Nicene Council. So books of the Bible were being judged to see if they were 'worthy' of being included in the official version of the Bible. So the *Gnostic Gospels* were hidden away, sealed in jars, and buried or hidden in caves, only to be discovered first in Nag Hammadi in 1945 CE. Why were they hidden? They were forbidden. It became dangerous to have them.

Gnostic Christians believe that humans contain a piece of the divine within their own being. Sound familiar? This idea was considered heresy for hundreds of years in Christianity. There is still a lively argument about it in the religion. Once you've studied eastern philosophy and gotten some personal experience of these states, even just a little taste, the teachings about enlightenment jump out at you when you return to your childhood tradition if that religion was Christian.

Here are a few examples from the New Testament: "Neither shall they say, 'Lo here! or, lo there!' for, behold, the kingdom of God is within you"(Luke 17:21). Christ tells us, "These things I have spoken unto you, that in me ye might have peace. In the world ye shall have tribulation: but be of good cheer; I have overcome the world." (John 16:33). In the Gospel of John there's more: "Verily, verily, I say unto you, He that believeth on me, the works that I do shall he do also; and greater works than these shall he do…" (John 14:12). "There was the true Light which, coming into the world, enlightens every man…" (John 1:9). (John was quite the mystic, don't you think?) "Let the same mind be in you that was in Christ." (Philippians 2:5). You get the idea.

Kabbalah, the mystical teachings of Judaism, lays out the structure of manifestation from the One Consciousness to the earth and at the same time teaches how to climb back up the Tree of Life to enlightenment. The Sufis are the metaphysical sect of Islam now, although some Egyptian Egyptologists (if you'll pardon the repetition) claim the Sufis are older than this newest Abrahamic religion, dating back into ancient Khemit (Egypt). Read any Rumi or Hafiz poem and you are being taught about enlightenment. Take this excerpt this Rumi poem:

> *Lo, I am with you always* means that when you look for God,
> God is in the look of your eyes,
> in the thought of looking, nearer to you than your self,
> or things that have happened to you
> There's no need to go outside.

Be melting snow.
Wash yourself of yourself.[5]

I am all orders of being, the circling galaxy, the
evolutionary intelligence, the lift, and the falling away.
What is, and what isn't.[6]

Hafiz writes,
A billion times God has turned a human back into Herself.
We all stand in line for the highest gift". [7]
You are the Sun in drag. You are God hiding from
yourself.[8]
The Gnostic Christians expressed a belief in reincarnation.
Hafiz even talks about the idea that after so many lives, we will
return home to the One Consciousness. Here are the opening lines
of "The Nile's End":
We are at
The Nile's end.
We are carrying particles
From every continent, creature, and age (lines 1-4)[9]
In the ancient Egyptian tradition, the Nile represented the
human spine and the temples along its banks were centers of power
aligned with certain Neters. Here it represents the long history of
the soul's journey in manifestation.

---

[5] Rumi. "Be Melting Snow," *The Essential Rumi*. Translated by
Coleman Barks, Harper San Francisco, 1995, 13

[6] Rumi, "Say I Am You," *The Essential Rumi*. Translated by Coleman Barks,
Harper San Francisco, 1995, 275.

[7] Hafiz, Back Into Herself," *The Gift*. Translated by Daniel Ladinsky,
Penguin, 1999, 131.

[8] Hafiz, "The Sun in Drag," *The Gift*. Translated by Daniel
Ladinsky, Penguin, 1999, 252.

[9] Haifz.. "Please," *The Gift*. Translated by Daniel Ladinsky, Penguin,
1999, 115.

The Western metaphysical traditions claim they originated in Egypt where the One Consciousness can be parallel with the Neter Neteru—the God of the gods—although my Egyptologist partner translates Neter as principle or aspect of the One Consciousness. As God manifests, different frequencies develop. Those frequencies of creation have a specific intelligence related to the level of creation that manifests from their seed. This was represented by an image. As consciousness waned when we fell from the Golden Age or Sat Yuga—The Age of Pure Knowledge—humans began to perceive these different Neters as separate gods and goddesses. Akhenaton tried to return Egypt to the understanding that all comes from and is contained in the Aten, the fourth stage of the sun representing full enlightenment. I'll circle back to these ages soon.

Western Metaphysics talks about enlightenment in terms of esoteric grades. We begin our spiritual work as a neophyte. We progress through the paths between the spheres on the Tree of Life. Gareth Knight lays out these levels in his opus, *A Practical Guide to Qabalistic Symbolism*. They are Zelator, Theoricus, Practicus, Philosophus, Adeptus Minor, Adeptus Major, Adepus Exemptus, Magister Templi, Magus, and finally Ipsissimus. This final state is merging with the top of the tree, Kether, the source of all manifestation or the One Consciousness.

The nature religions around the world have their medicine people, their priests and priestesses, who help people move into harmony through rituals and healing. Plant medicines or guides are often used to allow us to expand our consciousness and find the more cosmic levels.

What I've offered here are a very few examples. There are more examples in each of these spiritualities and more traditions beyond the ones I've mentioned, but if you listen carefully when you encounter any of them, you will hear the "intimations of immortality," as Wordsworth wrote, in them all. You will hear about the possibility of an end of suffering, of Unity.

What about gurus? In India, some traditions urge the student to surrender to the spiritual teacher. Many people think those of us who became involved with gurus in the 1970s were 'suckered' into cults. That we gave our power over to people who manipulated us. Recounting this experience, it is clear that the TM movement was not filled with enlightened people who were filled with compassion or were invariably kind. Was Maharishi himself enlightened? I can't answer this question. All I can say for certain is that my experience of Unity was real.

I learned a great deal in the TM movement, and meditating changed me for the better. I was dedicated and gave myself to it all fully. I wanted to believe the movement was bringing enlightenment to the world. This would include acceptance of me. But I wasn't accepted. I was inexperienced about so many things. I have since learned that Maharishi was not celibate himself. He had affairs with women on staff. There was even a child. The woman and her baby were supported, but not allowed back into the movement. I had no idea about any of this then and wouldn't have believed it. I had faith that Maharishi was in Unity Consciousness and the movement would bring the Age of Enlightenment to the world. My understanding of spirituality matured. I learned I had to walk my own path.

Some claim that people in India understand spiritual gurus differently than the young westerners who met them for the first time in the 1970s during the "guru invasion." The guru is a part of life in India, someone who teaches, advises, and perhaps oversees rituals in the temples. He is not someone who will make demands of complete obedience that would harm the student or expect a person to twist themselves into a pretzel to follow his teachings. This is not a true spiritual teacher and this is more readily understood in the East.

Humans are susceptible to cults. I heard someone being interviewed on the news the other night say that cults promise the fulfillment of our deepest dream and that it is very difficult to rationally see the group that has promised this. Is the TM movement a cult? Some say yes, others no. Is it possible for one person to experience an organization as a cult and another to be free in the same group? Perhaps. Ultimately, we all have to walk our own path. As a friend who is also a TM teacher said, "I keep my eyes on my own plate." The best definition of "guru" I've ever heard is that the guru is your Highest Self, the One Consciousness embodied in you.

I slowly left the TM movement behind starting in 1978. The last big course I attended was held in Amhurst. Maharishi had recently taught the siddhis. The word 'siddhis' refers to special abilities such as levitation or invisibility. This practice is based on the Patanjali sutras. At Amhurst, we meditated and did the siddhi program together in huge groups, which generated enormous spiritual energy.

I had a brief samadhi experience after I returned home. I lived in an apartment at the crest of Capitol Hill in Seattle with a view of Puget Sound and the mountains beyond it. As I gazed out at the water, I felt a deepening in the Sound and surrounding mountains. The water stirred within itself and seemed to turn a deeper blue. Then it changed into something deeper still. It melted into a pool of soft energy, an awareness that flowed up and out toward me, reaching for me with a joyous leap. The energy woke everything in its path, reaching into every nook and cranny of the land. Then it touched me, piercing my heart center. I actually felt physical pain.

We are one, the water whispered, *we are the same. Eternal, ever flowing.*

I am eternal. I am everything, I felt.

I was connected with everything around me. Then the experience stopped as suddenly as it had begun, leaving me standing in front of a dark, gaping cavern.

What in the hell is happening to me? I wondered.

Unity. My mind classified the experience automatically. Experience of self and world as universal consciousness, but these words gave no hint of that melting compassion and acceptance, of the ache of that exquisite beauty, of the sheer panic when it was suddenly gone.

At that moment, the kettle on the stove screamed and I jumped.

I didn't remember this experience when I first started working on this book, but after poking around in these memories, my brain served it up. When I first started writing, I didn't count it as another samadhi experience. I still don't. Maybe I didn't remember it because it happened so fast. The swell came up in me quickly but then dropped me back down just as fast. It was around this time that Maharishi started talking about the fear of enlightenment. A lot of people who'd gone to the Amhurst course were having a rough transition back to what is often called 'the real world.' Maharishi used to talk about it in terms of a river meeting the ocean. There is a moment of fear. The river feels it will be annihilated, lose its identity. But of course, it is the opposite that happens. The river becomes the ocean and maintains its sense of itself. Yet in my experience standing looking out at the Sound, I bounced back and felt the lack of fullness acutely.

I returned to the Center to do some group meditation to smooth out my transition from this powerful course. Other teachers were talking about how rough coming back was. Maharishi lectured on the fear of enlightenment, the panic the small self can feel right before it unites with the larger Self. I'd felt that joy before.

About a month later, I had another experience that sent me off to excavate this "dark, gaping cavern" I'd felt standing by the window when the great swell of pure consciousness receded. I got the flu. As the illness continued, I began to feel spectral, without substance. Then a thought intruded into my head.

I'm going to die.

I shook myself like a horse, throwing the thought off like water. It was ridiculous. I only had the flu.

I remember turning on the tiny TV perched on a crate and watching whatever presented itself for a while. But I felt worse. Why not go to bed early and sleep? Then I'd wake up ready for work tomorrow. I'd be into the week again and this would be over. I gathered up the tea pot, cups, and Kleenex that had proliferated around me, took them into the kitchen, then headed for bed. The sheets were cold at first. I put on socks, pulled my sweatshirt hood over my head, and waited for the bed to warm up. I lay, listening to my pulse in my ears, the monotonous beat of my life. I listened for my mantra and it picked up the rhythm. The clock ticked in the breakfast nook.

This is the end, I'm going to die. This is the end, I'm going to die began repeating itself in my head, over and over.

But I just have the flu, I argued back.

This is the end. This is the end repeated itself.

But I don't understand.

I fell asleep.

The next morning, my illness continued unabated as did the persistent thought and its counterargument.

I'm going to die.

I sank down lower into the bed. *I only have the flu. It's just lasting longer than usual.*

I listened to see how this thought was received as a person listens for a stone to strike the bottom of a well. The thought landed on a ledge of certainty—*I'm going to die*—and melted like snow on warm pavement.

I looked around my room at the bare linen walls, the smooth-running mahogany trim, the fern in the corner, the globe base of the lamp next to the bed with its two beige and brown wheat stalks. The room was almost empty, the afternoon sun offering a faint glow through the drawn blinds. The fern bent her lovely green head in acceptance and would not look up at me.

So, maybe I am going to die.

I was a little amused at the idea of dying from the flu. My aunt died of it during the flu epidemic in 1919. But my acceptance had shifted something deep underground. A thought began to float to the surface. I waited.

You must change. Completely. Or you will die.

I lay absolutely still, staring at the pale white ceiling in the afternoon gloom and considered this. I knew it was the truth, although I could never have explained it to anyone. I thought this was quite unfair. Was a bit offended by the whole thing. I'd been meditating seriously for years now. I took my spiritual evolution seriously. My parents had both died. My brother was in a mental hospital diagnosed with schizophrenia. I was basically alone in the world. Somehow though I knew that if I didn't make the change that was being demanded of me, I would meet with some accident or simply get sicker. I was on the brink of some transformation, a caterpillar about to enter a chrysalis, but I had no idea what was on the other side of this precipice. I lay silent.

Could I do it? Just agree without knowing what lay ahead? Without knowing why I had come to this end, why I had to change so drastically?

The silence continued, unrelenting, offering no answers and no escape.

"All right, I'll change," I said out loud.

I surrendered. Remember that?

Immediately, three faces appeared, staring down at me, concerned but serene. *She's ready now,* one said. The others nodded. Then the one who had spoken noticed that I could see him, and I felt his mild surprise. They looked into each other's eyes for a minute, then he was gone, as if a shade had been pulled down between them.

I wondered who they were. Guides? Would I see them again? But I knew it didn't matter. They would always be with me, whether I saw them or not. I felt myself drifting off.

So, it was decided. I had chosen. I would live and everything would be different now. I fell asleep.

And woke up well the next morning.

This wild experience led to me going into therapy. I asked around for recommendations and picked a Zen psychiatrist. A meditator going into therapy? Who ever heard of such a thing? Certainly not in the TM movement at that time. But that dark, gaping cavern had shown itself to me. In my first session, I explained that I was depressed.

My new therapist nodded, then asked, "So, what's wrong with being depressed?"

This guy is nuts, I thought.

He encouraged me to just feel depressed and not resist it. He was a Zen Buddhist, after all. This was my first serious experience with another spiritual system. It taught to be present to whatever presents itself. So I took him up on it. I felt my feelings. I allowed memories to surface. I spent about two years cleaning out this cavern. Not to say I finished the job in two years, but I was a much more balanced person afterward.

While I did this, I moved away from the TM movement. I discovered a lot of people in it were dedicated to denial. No 'negative' feelings were allowed. We were supposed to be enlightened, which is impossible I now knew without deep self-exploration. We can't ignore the personality that developed in our childhood. We can't hold our nose and wait for it to heal eventually. It will, but we'll have to live with it for a long while. That's a rough path. Apparently, my guides weren't going to let me take that road.

I moved on to graduate school and got my first university teaching job at The Evergreen State College in Olympia, Washington, where I was nominally head of the Center in the early 1980s. I didn't really see myself as being in the movement anymore. It took a lot of work to understand what had happened and become independent. I gradually started exploring other spiritual teachings and techniques, although I continued to meditate and still do. It's a foundational practice for me.

Once some meditators who were disenchanted with the movement tried to convince me I was addicted to the practice and that I should stop. I argued with them. Addiction brought destruction, I said. Meditation improved me in many ways. Perhaps I had been addicted to the movement. I saw it as the only path to enlightenment. That's why I titled my novel about it *God in a Box.* I believed the TM movement had the only key to enlightenment. I know now there is never only one way. There is a best way for each person, but if that way gets blocked, Mother Nature will show us another option. God is way too big to be put in a box.

This first awakening changed me in many ways. It left me with a certainty that enlightenment exists. I continued meditating and grew strong enough to face the deep wounds of my childhood and even past lives. Oddly enough, being a part of a meditation movement gave me the strength to step away and become self-sufficient, more independent in many ways. I expanded my spiritual horizons, using my own experience and intuition as a litmus test for what worked for me.

Which brings us to my second experience of an exalted state of consciousness, another experience that was not on my map of possibilities, even with all the training I'd gotten and all the meditating I was still doing.

CRYSTAL SKULLS

5

THE SECOND TIME I EXPERIENCED samadhi, I was sitting in front of
Max, the Crystal Skull, in a little town near Kona, Hawai'i. The
year was 1997. I had come to see this supposedly ancient Mayan
artifact. The spiritual center I was staying at during my vacation
was hosting Max. I thought the whole thing was pretty peculiar, to
tell the truth, but I'd developed a strong friendship with one of the
permanent residents of the place. She assured me Max was worth
spending some time with and I respected her opinion.

I attended the evening group meeting. Maybe ten to fifteen
people sat on pillows on the floor in a circle. The skull sat in the
middle on a slightly raised platform. At least I guess that's what
the bump under the shawl was. I took my place on a zafu, a
meditation pillow, and waited for the skull's keeper, JoAnn Parks,
to unveil him. JoAnn introduced Max and bent down to pull the

covering away. I briefly felt like I was attending a magic show and glanced over at my new friend with a bit of a frown. She gave a small shake of her head and smiled.

Me and Max
Photo by Stephen Mehler

The shawl came off and there sat Max—a crystal the shape and size of a human skull. Internal fractures ran through the stone and the lights danced off them, breaking into rainbows. A cloudy spot at the top of the skull and several more created around the back intriguing misty areas. JoAnn talked about how she'd come to be the skull's guardian— her daughter's tragic illness, and the Tibetan Red Hat healer who'd helped her live two more years with bone cancer. The healer was Max's previous guardian and passed the skull on to JoAnn at his death.

In her lecture, JoAnn moved on to technical information about how much Max weighed—eighteen pounds it turned out—and more scientific evidence about crystal, how it conducts energy, how crystal is used in computers and watches. She explained that the crystal Max had been carved from had seen at least two large earthquakes and endured enormous pressure before being quarried and carved. As she continued, I closed my eyes to listen. The scientific data, the measurements of the piece, didn't interest me as much as her personal story. Quite naturally, I drifted into meditation. I settled into a nice, quiet state, with JoAnn's story wafting over me.

Suddenly, a stream of energy flowed out to me from the skull. Surprised, I turned my attention to it. The stream of energy was like a knock on the door, as if Max were asking, "Can I come in?" Very polite. I gave him my permission, not in words so much as in a willingness. Then another experience that had not been on my map of possibilities occurred.

Max took that stream of energy he'd extended to me and opened it up into a firehose. He blasted me with a flood of extremely high-frequency energy. It pushed me back into myself and I lifted into a higher state of consciousness.

Christ Consciousness. My mind labeled the experience, but that was not a label I'd learned anywhere.

It seemed Max had a direct link to Christ Consciousness and he'd opened the door for me. I didn't walk so much as get blasted through.

As soon as I connected with my full Self, I began to weep. Right there in the middle of all those other people. I couldn't stop. I cried because I'd given up ever experiencing enlightenment again in this lifetime. This was such a relief. Such a surprise. I felt a rush of joy. All the pain, loneliness, and confusion I'd been carrying washed away with that roaring influx of Christ Consciousness.

I cried for a good while. JoAnn walked over and put her hand on my shoulder while she talked. I tried to be quiet, but I couldn't bring myself to suppress my crying because I didn't want to lose my connection. At last, my weeping subsided, and I sat within the golden sunlight of that experience, full and healed.

Now don't get me wrong, now. It's not like I thought I was Christ. I had been uplifted into communion with this level of awareness that Max understood as Christ Consciousness. Somewhere in the midst of this experience, I stopped thinking of Max as an object and realized he was a conscious being. A very advanced conscious being.

This time I didn't worry much about when it would fade. I was under no illusions that I was pure enough to sustain this level permanently, although I would have dearly loved that. But since I was inside it now, these thoughts didn't even come to me. I just enjoyed the relief of being home again.

My meditation with Max happened toward the end of my trip to Hawai'i. I'd treated myself to this vacation after leaving a shamanic study group I'd been heavily involved with. There were the usual power struggles and squabbles, and the group had become more contentious.

The teacher had been trained in the Hopi tradition. The Hopi are quite a secretive group. They don't share their inner teachings with outsiders. There are a few rare exceptions. If I left his group, I knew I could never learn this history or these rituals. Their history reached back for millennia. We were supposedly in the fourth world, getting ready to break into the fifth. I wanted to know more. Here was a living tradition, much like the Vedic one.

The loss of this teacher and this group was similar to my walking away from the TM movement. I felt this was the only door to this knowledge. But the conflict disrupted the rituals so much that I decided it was best for me to leave. I was not entirely innocent in all this. I see now how I contributed, but at the time I didn't see any other way to resolve the situation.

I mourned the loss for a couple of months and then treated myself to a trip to Hawai'i as a rite of passage. I moved from one part of my life into the future, whatever it might hold. When I landed in Hawai'i, the land spoke to me. This place was *alive*. When I hiked in the Hawai'i Volcanoes National Park, I laid out a medicine wheel in a secluded area. Pele talked to me while I was at work, mentioning how I'd always lived near a mountain range.

It's no accident your name is Crater, she said.

After my meditation with Max, the experience of Christ Consciousness gradually faded over the evening and the next morning. However, it dramatically changed my life. My senses were tuned to a fine point. I remember driving home from the airport to Manitou Springs, where I lived at the time. I could

80

pinpoint the state patrol officers who were out in force for some reason. They felt like balls of buzzy, chaotic energy. My radar seemed to extend farther than theirs, so it was easy to slow down before I reached them.

I came home knowing that I was supposed to move to Boulder. Max didn't tell me. My guides didn't whisper it in my ear. I just knew. I had no doubts about it. I made arrangements to sell my little cottage above the Cog Railway that ran up to Pikes Peak and moved into a rental in my new town. As soon as I got unpacked, I got a copy of the local weekly, and guess what I discovered?

Max was coming to Boulder.

Now my guides piped up. I was told my experience with Max would not be as intense this time, but I wanted to go anyway. I befriended the woman who was hosting JoAnn and the skull, helping her organize a bit. On Friday afternoon, I'd scheduled a private meditation with Max. I arrived filled with anticipation, even though I'd been warned against expecting too much. As soon as I walked into the room, I felt Max surround me with love. I burst into tears before the person who'd ushered me in had a chance to say anything. He left and I sat down in front of this beautiful being, the reflected candlelight creating flickers of color shimmer inside him.

I started to ask him questions. The first one was about a relationship. I'd been in a relationship for a good while with the naturopath I mentioned earlier. We'd both just finished graduate school when we met. I got a job in Olympia and she decided to open her professional office there. We went through imposter syndrome together. Each morning I'd say, "I'm going to go pretend to be a college professor now." She would reciprocate with "I'm going to go pretend to be a doctor now." We'd laugh and go off to work. About two or three months in, we stopped saying the pretend part. We moved into our new roles in life. We bought a house. We were good in many ways, in some ways not.

Olympia is one of the rainiest and moldiest places in the very wet Pacific Northwest. We had decided to move to Colorado for her health. She needed to live in a dryer climate. The move exacerbated the ways we were not good together and after some couples' therapy, we separated. I dove deeply into my spirituality again, joining the shamanic study group. I am aware of the controversy around this word, which comes from the Steppes of Russia and is not a traditional Native American term. Because my group was eclectic, it fit best.

My inherent psychic abilities developed much more deeply with this study. My mother was psychic. Most of her sisters were to some extent. It seemed to run in the family. With some cultivation, mine blossomed more fully. Eastern meditations don't focus on developing these abilities. Just do the meditation and everything unfolds naturally from there.

Western spiritual traditions tend to work with the subtle levels of creation, with finding our spirit guides and nature connections, in learning to paying attention to dreams. I've sometimes said that the East starts with the One Consciousness, letting the aspirant purify more and more as they attune to the vibrations of the mantra or chants. The Kabbalistic Western tradition I studied started in the here and now, at the bottom of the Tree of Life, and systematically climbed up to the top.

By the time I saw Max in Boulder, I'd been told by guides that my next relationship would be with a man. I was bi-sexual, but had been with women since 1970. It was now into the 1990s. My guides showed me an image of him—just a flash, so I didn't really get any details. I wouldn't have recognized him, but I was open to this possibility. I wasn't desperately waiting, though. Sitting in front on Max in Boulder in 1997, I asked about this relationship. It was a year overdue if I could count on my guides' timing. I've often been told beings on the less physical planes are notoriously bad with timing.

When I started asking questions, Max shushed me. He told me I knew better than to waste time with such inquiries, that I knew what was important. Raising my frequency. Reaching that state he'd catapulted me into in Hawai'i, even if I'd been told I wouldn't get there this time.

I heard his voice in my head. *Put your forehead on mine.*

82

So I did and we spent the half hour with Max "buzzing" me with energy. I was definitely more clear and calm after the session. I was definitely not in Christ Consciousness.

I've recently learned that the pineal gland contains piezoelectric crystals. These crystals can generate an electric charge, emitting light, when exposed to pressure. One way to create this pressure is through sound. Crystal skulls tend to activate more when a person puts their hands on either side and applies just a bit of pressure. The pineal gland crystals respond to sound and it seems obvious to me to crystal. The gland also sends energy out. The pineal gland interacts with crystal skulls and the sound from crystal bows, mantras, and chanting, producing the chemicals in the brain that assist with higher consciousness. Max told me to put my forehead next to him, the site of the pineal gland. Mayan legend holds that as we approach enlightenment, our bones turn more and more from calcium-based to crystalline.

I was scheduled to do the group meditation that evening, so I stayed for a potluck supper my friend had organized. People started arriving, bringing their contributions. My ex came with her new girlfriend, driven by curiosity. Some crystal dealers from Colorado Springs arrived, along with a guy who carried a briefcase of all things. This amused me for some reason. He put down his briefcase and we all filled our plates, settling in different spots to eat. I sat next to the briefcase guy and asked him what he was into.

"Egypt," he said and talked a bit about his trip there. "And you?"

"I'm more interested in the Maya right now."

We chatted. Other people joined us in the living room, and soon JoAnn set up for her lecture. We sat around in a circle again. JoAnn gave a shorter talk this time since several people in the group knew Max's background. Apparently, the Egypt enthusiast was also a crystal skull expert. He'd done research on some skulls when he served as a staff research scientist for the Rosicrucian Order in San Jose.

After JoAnn wound up her talk, she invited each of us to sit in front of Max for a few minutes. She started to invite the first person up, then paused and stared at Max. After a few seconds, she turned to my ex and said, "I guess Max wants you to go first."

We settled into silence, some meditating, all waiting for our turn. I was about halfway around the circle. The crystal dealers both took a turn. I discovered later the woman in this couple was an old TM teacher. Then the Egypt guy who was sitting next to me scooted up. He did some fancy gestures over Max, then put his brow down on the skull, third eye to third eye, just as Max had instructed me to do earlier.

After a few seconds, Max "turned" to me—that's what it felt like—and he asked, *Will this one do?*

Max with Stephen Mehler the night I met him
Photo by Joe Swanson

I was flabbergasted. Was Max playing matchmaker? Was this the guy I'd seen in that visionary flash? I decided to trust Max's judgment and get to know him. We exchanged numbers. His name was Stephen Mehler. I was in a counseling program at Colorado University Colorado Springs at the time. The next time I traveled down for a class, we went out on a date. We continued to see each other. I think we were sitting on a bluff in Palmer Park when I confessed that Max had suggested him to me.

"I've heard of crystal skulls doing that before," he said. "They've done that with me."

I was a bit put off by this reaction, to tell the truth. Why wasn't he still with this woman, I wondered.

"What did Max say?" Stephen asked.

"He asked me if you would do," I said, putting a bit of unnecessary emphasis on the last word.

Stephen laughed. He reached over and squeezed my hand, which helped me forgive him. Then he confessed, "When you said you weren't interested in Egypt, I thought that this would never work out." But it did. Stephen and I have been together since. He moved in with me in Boulder the next year, after my cats' approval of course. In 1999, he took me to Egypt for the first time and the energy of the land and monuments won me over.

✦✦✦

We landed at the Cairo airport late at night and packed onto a bus for the trek across the city to our hotel at the Giza plateau. We dropped our guide off near his house, a block away from the Sphinx and pyramids. But it was dark and I couldn't really see anything. Stephen went into a store with the others to buy water, which was way less expensive than what the hotel would charge. I walked over to the wall separating tourists from the plateau. I squinted into the dark and made out the conical head of the Sphinx.

"She's smaller than I imagined," I said to the person standing next to me.

He agreed, but from the dark came a voice. *Just wait until I get ahold of you,* I heard her say.

Me & the Sphinx in 1999
Photo by Stephen Mehler

The Sphinx, Sekhmet, Egypt—they all got a strong hold on me.
I'll tell you more about how the land speaks to us later.

Stephen and I got married in the Hathor Temple in Dendera
during that tour. His ex, who was a Martinist priestess, did the
honors. It wasn't how we'd planned it, but that's Egypt. Make
plans and watch them get thrown up in the air and blown away.
But she did a great job, ignoring the antiquity guards who kept
yelling for us to get on the bus while we were in the middle of the
ceremony. We kept it brief and I didn't mind one bit.

Stephen shared more than crystal skulls with me. Shortly after
we met, he gave me Drunvalo Melchizedek's material, which I
read with interest. I had not learned anything about sacred
geometry before. Stephen did talks on Egypt and crystal skulls at
various conferences, and I went with him. Not academic
conferences, like I was used to, but more alternative history and
New Age groups.

The first one I attended with him was a UFO conference. I went with some skepticism, even though my mother had claimed to see a UFO when I was a child. Before she told me about her alien craft encounter, I distinctly remember sitting at the kitchen table while she read a newspaper article to me about how a UFO had been discovered. The Roswell crash happened in 1947. I was born in 1950, so it must have been an incident in the early 1950s. I was quite small. I remember sitting in the chair kicking my legs which were a long way from reaching the floor. Perhaps it was the 1953 incident in Kingman, Arizona, although I would have been going on two that summer and we were in the house my father built in 1954. I would have been too young. This was more likely an event a couple of years later.

She read the account and I listened with rapt attention. Mother kept glancing up at me as she read. When she finished, she set the paper down, took a drink of coffee, then said, "So beings from another planet have visited us."

"What are they like?" I asked. This discovery excited me.

She picked up her coffee cup again, then eyed me over the rim. "Doesn't that scare you?"

"No."

"It scares some people."

"Why?"

"Because they might be really different than us. More powerful."

I just shook my head.

"They're afraid the aliens might try to hurt us."

"Why would they do that?"

"Do you think they would try to hurt us?"

I shook my head. "I want to know what they look like."

In a couple of days, we were back at the kitchen table. Mother was reading the newspaper and drinking coffee. She sat up straighter and snapped the paper so she could fold it over. I had a burning desire to learn how to do that. When I tried, I always just crumpled it up.

"Says here the government claims there were no aliens. That the remains of the ship were just a weather balloon that crashed." She read the article to me.

I frowned and shook my head.

"What do you think?" she asked.

"That doesn't make any sense."

Mother unpacked my thoughts for me since I didn't quite have the words to express what I was feeling. "A spaceship wouldn't look anything like a weather balloon, right?"

"That's right."

"Their description of a weather balloon doesn't match the report a few days ago. I don't believe this," she said. "Do you?"

"No. But ..." Again, words failed me.

"Why would the government make up a story like this?"

I nodded.

"I think they're just trying to calm people down."

"But I wanted to see them."

"Who?"

"The people from outer space."

A few years later—I was perhaps eight or nine—my mother saw a UFO up close. One Saturday afternoon, she came home very excited from a drive to Gastonia where some of her family lived. She walked into the kitchen and put her purse on the counter. "You wouldn't believe what I saw on my way home," she said, a bit breathless.

"What?'

"A UFO."

"Really?" I squealed. "What did it look like?"

She shook her head, still in disbelief. "It was like some big metal thing with layers." She stretched her hands out and up, trying to give me an idea.

"Was it round?" That's what they looked like on TV.

"No, it was square or like a rectangle. It just hung in the air next to the road. Several of us stopped to look at it."

My eyes were the size of the saucers I was imagining. "Did you see any aliens?"

"No," she said, then gave a shy laugh. "I was kinda scared, so I'm sort of glad I didn't."

Then I made a big mistake. I told people the next morning at church that my mother had seen a UFO. After the service, a woman walked up to my family and asked me, "Theresa, you said your mother saw a UFO." Her voice dripped with sarcasm, which didn't register with me at first.

"She did," I said at the same time my mother gasped out, "Don't be ridiculous."

"Well, your child said you saw one."

"She's just confused about something we saw on television," Mother said.

"But momma, you said—"

"Now, Theresa, stop making up stories."

"But—" I began, at which point Mother grabbed my arm and pulled me down the aisle saying, "You need to stop making up stories."

I was baffled. What had I done wrong?

In the car, she exploded. "I can't believe you don't have any more sense than to tell those people I saw a UFO."

"But you did."

"Of course I did, but they don't believe in UFOs. They'll think I'm crazy."

"But . . ." This time I couldn't figure out what to say.

"Most people don't believe in them. The government has put out a lot of stories to discredit anyone who's seen one." She stared at me for a minute. "Honestly, I don't know what gets into you sometimes. Just never tell anybody else, OK?"

I agreed, quite subdued.

Imagine my surprise when around 2015 or so I was driving home from work on Highway 36 and saw a rectangular, boxy structure hovering next to a field. One car had pulled off the freeway onto the side road to check it out. I saw what looked like stairs descending from the larger structure. I kept wanting to pull off the highway and go see it, but for some reason, I never worked up the nerve. I think it was the stairs. Were they going to come down them? Did they want us to climb up?

No other cars arrived at the strange metal box hanging in the sky. Did they just rationalize that it was some machine for construction, even if it was just hovering right above the ground? Did they not see it at all? Or were they scared of it like I was, much to my disappointment? I'll never know. I looked for it again for a couple of days, even though I knew it was unlikely to show up again.

Given these experiences, I was not prepared to dismiss all the people at the UFO conference as kooks, even though a few of them were. Most people gave reasoned, well-documented presentations—some in that dry, plodding manner of engineers, others with a bit more flare. I joked later that a couple seemed to be out on a day pass from their institution.

Stephen's talk started with the commonly held belief that the pyramids were built by aliens. He and his Egyptian mentor, Abdel Hakim Awyan, rejected this notion. Stephen explained the idea of ages or yugas, as they're called in the Vedas. His contention was that during the Golden Age when people were in full consciousness, they had mastery over these gigantic blocks of stone.

In indigenous Khemitian teachings, five is an important number. There are five stages of the sun or day, people have five names, etc. In this context, there are five ages that correspond to the five stages of the sun. These roughly correspond to the four yugas in Vedic teachings. The Egyptian full cycle lasts 65,000 years, but a full yuga cycle, or maha yuga, lasts 4,320,000 years. These numbers obviously don't match up, but the idea of human consciousness waxing and waning is similar.

The Maya have a similar cycle, which gave rise to the common misperception that the world would end along with one of the Maya calendars in 2012. Their calendars are like Russian dolls, shorter ones fitting into longer ones fitting into even longer one. I'm not expert enough in the Maya cycle to explain it in any detail, but you'll find similar ideas of humanity being very conscious and good prevailing followed by times when evil deeds and darkness rule.

The first stage in Egyptian lore is Kheper (the Driller), represented by the scarab beetle. Everyone's seen this image in Egyptian iconography. This insect lays its eggs in a ball of dung. When the babies hatch, they have a food source. You can still walk along in Egypt and occasionally run across one of these beetles pushing a ball of dung. This represents morning, the rising sun, and also the first age. Humans are starting to wake up from the long night. In Vedic lore, this stage is most similar to the end of Kali Yuga turning into Dvapara Yuga, when humanity is beginning to rouse from a dull state of consciousness.

The second stage of the sun at high noon is Ra (the Stubborn). This comes as a surprise to many because Ra is often seen as the sun god. Here Ra, the ram, represents the adolescent, who is stubbornly certain of his knowledge. The Vedic yuga that most corresponds with this is Dvapara Yuga. The teaching of this age emphasizes compassion and truthfulness. Humanity is waking up. The spiritual teachers of this age are said to only understand half of the Vedas.

The third stage of the sun is Oon (the Wise). This is early afternoon and in terms of the ages represents a time when humanity has attained wisdom. The symbol for this state is a mature man walking with a staff. Treta Yuga corresponds with this stage when humanity has reached a more heightened state of consciousness. The bull of dharma standing on three legs symbolizes this yuga—not fully balanced, but getting there.

The fourth stage in Khemitology is Aten or Iten (the Wiser), the late afternoon. During this time, humanity enjoys the full flowering of consciousness, living in a state of enlightenment. We are masters of the world, understanding the laws of nature and using them in harmony with our surroundings. Aten is represented by an old man hunched over a staff. Sat Yuga is the time of enlightenment in the Vedic system. Here the bull of dharma stands on four legs showing balance. 'Sat' means pure knowledge. Humanity is living in full consciousness and in harmony with all.

This is the time we seem to have a cellular memory of the time we all yearn for, the time we call the Golden Age.

The fifth stage of the sun in Khemitian lore is Amen. This is a time of darkness. The sun has set. Humanity has fallen from consciousness and our actions are no longer in harmony with universal law. Corruption reigns. There is no image for this time. This is paralleled in Vedic teaching as Kali Yuga. Thankfully, Kali Yuga is the shortest of the periods while Sat Yuga is the longest. Unfortunately, we're in Kali Yuga now. Some say we're smack in the middle, which is downright depressing. Others say we're right at the end and can expect the light to dawn at any time. Enlightened teachers do incarnate during these times to rekindle the light of the One Consciousness for a time. The same terms are used to explain the stages of the day and the unfolding ages of human development. The basic concepts are the same.

Stephen and Hakim taught that the pyramids were built during a time of Aten. Yes, 'a' time rather than 'the' time because, just like the yugas, this is a never-ending cycle. Humans understood how to lift stones weighing many tons by levitation. Stephen knew Hakim was the indigenous elder he'd been looking for when he met him in 1992 in front of the Sphinx, named Tefnut in the old tradition. Hakim blandly stated that she—yes, she, the image of the Great Mother—was built 52,000 years ago. Stephen looked at him, then at the Sphinx, and she said, *This is the man you've been looking for.*[10]

---

[10] For more information on the indigenous teachings about Egypt/Khemit, see Mehler's book *The Land of Osiris*.

Stephen and Hakim at Beni Hasan
Photo by Patricia Awyan

Now let's get back to aliens and the UFO conferences. Stephen would teach these folks that humans in the full bloom of our consciousness built the pyramids, but that during these times we were also in touch with beings from the stars. This confused some people. Which was it? Did he believe in aliens or not? He answered, "Yes." The Egyptians were in communication with other star systems and Egyptians built the pyramids. Stephen would go on to talk about Ptah, how his name was "the one who pops from the blue through the waters from the sky." The blue and the sky indicate the stars to the old civilization. Perhaps Ptah came from another planet. This Egyptian Neter is most associated with Sirius.

The Dogon, an African tribe to the south of Egypt, knew about Sirius B hundreds of years before astronomers saw it. The Dogon have a legend that a spaceship landed in a lake in their area and sea creatures swam out. Stephen's favorite tale about the Dogon is their claim about cannabis. Ganja was a gift from the star people. It's an extraterrestrial plant.

Whatever the truth of this claim, people all over the globe have stories of people who came from the stars. The Inca told long tales about the cities under the Andes built by people fleeing the destruction of Mu, but the people who built Mu? You got it. Star people. At a crystal skull conference attended by several Mayan Daykeepers, Don Alejandro shared a teaching with us about how the Pleiadean star elders came to the planet and landed in four different places, one of them in Mexico and another in Egypt. He drew a map which Stephen still has. It connects to a site near Saqqara where Mayan glyphs decorate the ceiling of the tomb of a man named—you guess it again—Maya.

During one of the UFO conferences, a big group went out into the desert to look for flying saucers. We did see what looked like a star traveling in a line across the sky, then jumping to another place and traveling a ways, then jumping again. It zigzagged for a good half an hour. We thought maybe this was a UFO. Later people claimed it was the space station we were looking at.

Back in my TM days when I was cleared to go back to the teacher training course, our group stayed temporarily at a hotel in the French Alps while waiting to travel to our final destination. A story was circulating that the summer course had been visited by UFOs. I remember one night standing outside and someone pointing out where the ships would hover. I never saw one, but recently we watched a special on UFOs, *Close Encounters of the Fifth Kind*, that focused on Dr. Steven Greer's work. In the film, a woman talks about being on a teacher training course and how she saw a tetrahedron shaped craft hovering just above the tree line. Same place.

Dr. Steven Greer founded the Center for the Study of Extraterrestrial Intelligence (CSETI). Greer says that ETs are focused on raising our consciousness rather than all the other ideas expounded in films and conspiracy theories. They are not a danger. They are not interested in world domination. They seem to be interested in saving our planet by raising human awareness. In the show, Greer talked about seeing spaceships and hearing extraterrestrials speaking to him telepathically while he was on a

TM teacher training course in the French Alps. I realized this was the hotel I'd stayed in. While I was going to a course, he was just finishing his up.

Dr. Greer's protocol for communicating with ETs involves meditation. It starts with about thirty minutes to settle the mind into an expanded state. Then the person invites a UFO to visit. This involves sending mental images of where the person is, starting wide and by stages, focusing in on the exact location. Once Dr. Greer said he sent images of Charlotte, where he grew up, then details about where he was in the Appalachian Mountains to the northwest. That day, many people reported seeing UFOs in Charlotte and some were captured on film

According to his research, visitors from other star systems are interested in helping humans achieve higher states of consciousness. They have only interfered with human endeavors by disabling weapons systems that would have potentially set off mass explosions. Otherwise, extra-terrestrials commune with humans when we are in deep states of meditation or a state of love and harmony. Participants have reported telepathic connections and even healings.

Dr. Greer's involvement with the TM movement exposed him to Maharishi's siddhi program during which meditators were taught techniques to enhance special abilities (*siddhis* in Sanskrit). Some of these involve skills like increasing compassion to fancy stuff like levitation and invisibility. I heard reports of learning to walk through a solid object, although I never learned this technique. But Dr. Greer hypothesizes that alien propulsion is driven more by advanced consciousness than physical technology. Perhaps that they've linked these two together. He believes aliens might use *siddhis* to travel instantaneously from one point to another.

Quantum physics has demonstrated that consciousness has an effect on matter. There's the experiment where it seemed subatomic particles waited for the person to think which box they wanted for them to appear in before they arrived. Thought-guided action. The Heisenberg Effect holds that observing or measuring alters the phenomenon being observed. Again, awareness affects matter.

Dr. Masaru Emoto did experiments with projecting emotion into water. The water created beautiful, harmonious shapes with positive emotions, and chaotic, unappealing shapes with negative ones. It's long been accepted by many that awareness and the manifest world are not really separate from each other.

Physicists talk about entrained particles which are somehow linked. No matter how far apart they are, when one is affected by something, the other immediately changes as well. These entrained particles can pop from one place to another thousands of miles away instantaneously. Einstein called it "spooky action at a distance." Quite a formal name, don't you think? Dr. Greer believes UFOs that seem to phase in and out of materiality and appear in a different spot instantaneously use the qualities of quantum particles, even though quantum physics applies to things on the atomic level and these ships are much bigger.

Most of all, he talks about aliens wanting humanity to grow through our current challenges and evolve into a higher state. Dr. Greer repeatedly says no humans have ever been harmed during contact. He claims that alien abductions, strange surgeries, cow mutilations are staged by humans. He discusses a project run by international governments to make us afraid of star visitors. His evidence is quite extensive.

What do star people want with us? He reports on a meeting between an ET and an army officer. The ET is encouraging humans to communicate with his civilization. The officer asked, "What's in it for me?"

"A new world," the ET answered.

Dr. Greer believes they want the earth to evolve and join the enlightened galactic civilizations.

6

DURING THE FIRST COUPLE OF years of our relationship, Stephen shared a lot of the information he'd gathered in his life. We didn't have to explain our meditation practices to each other, though. One interesting synchronicity was Stephen's job when we first met. He basically worked for the TM movement in the Maharishi Ayurved business. He didn't do the meditation technique, however. He'd been initiated into Surat Shabd Yoga in 1988 before he moved to Colorado, another mantra meditation in the Vedic tradition.

Stephen was also a Rosicrucian and had worked in the 1980s as a staff research scientist for the Rosicrucian Order AMORC in San Jose. I heard some funny stories about this temple and office complex. Stephen used to go to weekly chanting there. They had a theatre and a group of his friends put on a series of plays in the Francis Bacon Auditorium on the premises. Ralph Lewis served as the Imperator of the Rosicrucian Order during World War II, but the world leadership passed back to France after things settled down.

Lewis lived across the street in a house that was later rented by one of Stephen's friends, Françoise Beaudoin. Under her proprietorship, the house earned the nickname of the Home for Lost Souls and Wayward Mystics. An eclectic group rented rooms from her. Françoise ran the Ram Metaphysical Bookstore for years with the assistance of a long line of entitled cats.

One story goes that Lewis' secretary would call him at his house to tell him there was a visitor for him in the waiting room just outside his office. He would say, "I'll be there in a minute." In a few minutes, he would call his secretary from inside his office and invite his visitor in. Nobody saw him cross the street, walk through the grounds, enter Rosicrucian headquarters, or walk through his waiting room. How did he get there? A secret tunnel connected the house and headquarters that ran under Naglee Street. The story goes that street repairs destroyed the tunnel.

Back to crystal skulls! In 1980 while Stephen worked for the Order, a man named John Zamora bought a crystal skull there in hopes the museum would purchase it. He was acting as an agent for a Maya priest named Francisco Reyes whose village was in dire poverty. They didn't want to part with their artifact, but they were starving. It fell to Stephen to study the skull in order to authenticate it. This first skull came to be known as the Mayan Crystal Skull, a cloudy quartz weighing close to nine pounds, smaller than Max.

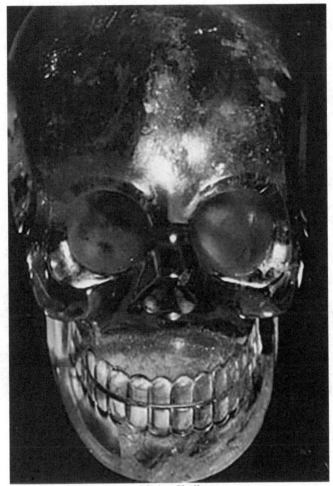

Mayan Skull
Photo by Stephen Mehler

A couple of years later, Zamora bought an amethyst skull to the museum. Stephen fell in love with this skull. By this time, he was no longer with the Order, but was still able to study it. He used both objective scientific techniques and psychometry sessions with a number of sensitives, as they're called by the Order, with both the Mayan and amethyst artifacts. Nick Nocerino also participated, a man who was widely known as the 'dean' of crystal skulls. Stephen provided detail about these skulls and others he's worked with in his book on crystal skulls, written with David Hatcher Childress.[11] He shared these stories and photos of the artifacts with me during the early years of our relationship. Then we went on to meet more skulls.

Stephen Mehler with Amethyst Skull
Photo by Françoise Beaudoin

---

[11] Childress, David Hatcher & Stephen S. Mehler. *The Crystal Skulls: Astonishing Portals to Man's Past.* Adventures Unlimited Press, 2008.

Nick Nocerino doing psychic reading with Amethyst Skull
Photo by Françoise Beaudoin

JoAnn's story about her journey with Max also involved Nick Nocerino. Max told JoAnn about Nick, not by name, but just calling him "the man." The Tibetan healer wanted to pass Max on to JoAnn Parks after he died. When this happened, she had no clear idea what to do with the skull, so she put him in a box in her closet. But that didn't stop Max from visiting her in her dreams and talking to her during the day.

"We're going to travel and see hundreds of people," he told her.

"You're nuts," was her answer.

"I'm important to mankind," he said.

She'd start to answer, then say to herself, "I'm talking to a rock."

Max kept at her. One day on television, JoAnn found a program on crystal skulls. She was astonished to see another artifact just like the one in a box up in her closet. The program host interviewed an expert on the subject, and while the man was talking, she heard Max saying from the box in the closet, "That's the man!" JoAnn called the local TV station and talked to someone about the show. "I have one of those," she said.

They laughed at her. But JoAnn was persistent and got the name of the expert and a way to contact him.

His name was Nick Nocerino. She called and told him about seeing his interview on the program and that she had a crystal skull. He didn't believe her either.

She persisted.

"Describe it," Nick said.

"It's a crystal with a face carved on it. It has one of those Jewish hats on top." (JoAnn was a Lutheran housewife in Texas and didn't know the lingo.)

Nick was quiet for a few seconds. Then he said, "You have the skull with the white cap?"

"Yes, that's what I'm telling you."

"I've been looking for that skull for years."

Nick flew out to Texas to meet Max and that was that, as they say. He and JoAnn worked together for a long while until Nick's passing in 2004.

I first met Nick at Chet and Kallista Snow's crystal skull conference in Sedona in 1998. Stephen and I had the opportunity to meet Nick's ancient skull, ShaNaRa. Nick named this skull after one of his guides. We were invited for private meditation with ShaNaRa. Nick asked Stephen to sit in front of the skull and I sat behind her. The back of this skull was filled with interesting inclusions and fractures with lots of opportunities for scrying, but I couldn't dive in. It felt impolite to do this without first saying hello, so I waited until Stephen was ready to let me take his seat. ShaNaRa said hello, then we dove in. I don't remember exactly what I saw that day. Maybe some past lives, but no big revelations. During that meditation, the skull felt feminine. I've seen it other times when it feels masculine. For convenience, I usually call this skull "she."

I'm not much of a scryer. Scrying is looking into a crystal or bowl of water in order to see visions. To do this, first start by paying attention to your breath. Don't try to change it. Just notice it. Then spend a couple of minutes meditating. Use whatever technique you prefer.

Set your intention. If you have a specific question, bring that into your awareness. Or you can just ask to see what is important at this time. If you're working with a skull, you can ask what it has to share with you. Open your eyes and look at the surface of the crystal or water. Allow your vision to get a little blurry and sink just beneath the surface. Be patient and see what starts to form. If you're working with a crystal ball or skull, it might help to touch the surface. As an empath, I find physical contact sends me a lot of information. You may have the same experience. As I said, I'm not very good at this. I usually see things in my head and not in the crystal or water. But I do start as I've suggested here. Scrying is described in a lot of books and on websites.

Nick's lecture at the Snow's conference was informative, and it was fun to spend time around him. He had a wicked sense of humor. JoAnn always seems to have something new to add to her lecture. She keeps researching and learning. Both Max and ShaNaRa were present at the 1998 conference. The two of them were in a room together and small groups were invited in to spend time with the skulls. I didn't have any particularly powerful experiences this time. I always feel clearer and more peaceful after spending time with skulls. We did see the northern lights during this event—not in the skulls, but in the skies of Sedona, Arizona! That was quite unexpected and everyone took it as a positive sign for the shift toward higher consciousness for the world.

Nick Nocerino & Stephen Mehler
Photo by Theresa Crater

Chet hosted more crystal skull conferences and then Kendall Ray Morgan did a series of them. Through these conferences and our own travels, I've met quite a few skulls, some ancient, some around one hundred or so years old, and others more contemporary. I connected very deeply with some, others not so much.

DaEl and Laurie Walker brought three old or ancient skulls to one of the Snow's conferences, Rainbow, Madre, and Zar. I fell in love with Madre. She seemed like an ancient skull to me, although I can't offer any objective proof. She was well named, giving off all-encompassing love and wisdom.

Madre, Rainbow, and Zar
Photo by Stephen Mehler

Kendall Ray Morgan introduced a previously unknown ancient skull at two of his conferences. The first one we attended was the 10-10-10 conference held in New York. Many skulls were in attendance, including some brought by the Mayan Daykeepers Hunbatz Men and Don Alejandro.

Don Alejandro at the U.N.
Photo by Stephen Mehler

Hunbatz Men
Photo by Stephen Mehler

Kendall's big reveal in 2010 was Einstein, whose keeper is Carolyn Ford. Stephen and I had a small booth at the back of the conference room. Carolyn came onto the stage with Einstein sitting on a table beneath a cloth cover, just like JoAnn had done with Max in Hawai'i. Carolyn spoke for a while about how she came to have the skull and how she'd invited Nick Nocerino to examine him. Stephen reminded me of the story Nick had shared, that there were other skulls kept privately by their owners. He considered Einstein a master skull, but Nick never revealed the name, where it was, or who had it.

When Carolyn took the covering off Einstein, his energy was so powerful that it pulled me straight up out of my chair. His image was also reflected off the windows in a building across the street, so he seemed to be surrounding us. This skull was so potent that it was difficult to articulate what I was experiencing. I didn't get to see him up close or privately, but we were able to visit Carolyn in Sedona when she invited Stephen to examine him. I wasn't able to get any private time with Einstein. Carolyn was kind enough to give me a reading using her system. Sometimes it's a challenge for me to tune into skulls when there's a lot going on around them, and this was the case for me during that visit.

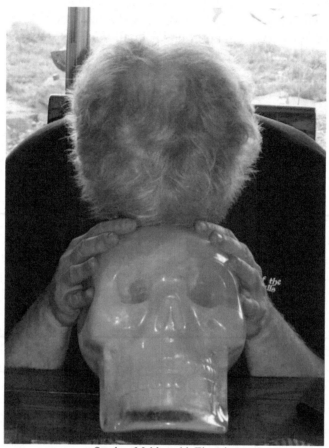

Stephen Mehler with Einstein
Photo by Theresa Crater

I did get a sense of what Nick Nocerino meant by saying
Einstein is a master skull. He is larger than the human-sized skulls,
measuring ten inches from front to back and weighing thirty-three
pounds. But his size is not the reason Einstein is a master skull.
Readers may be familiar with the legend of the thirteen crystal
skulls. The story goes that when the thirteen original skulls are
brought together, the earth will shift into an enlightened age.
Twelve skulls sit in a circle with a larger, master skull in the
middle of the circle, receiving the energy from the other skulls and

mediating that energy out to the world or the people participating in any ritual.

This is a wonderful story and certainly is one way the skulls would be arranged in a ceremony. Twelve and thirteen are important numbers. We have twelve disciples and the master Yeshua ben Yousef, or Jesus, making thirteen. There are twelve astrology signs with a hidden master thirteenth, Ophiuchus, the activation point for our neighborhood in the galaxy. While in Hawai'i, I had a dream about how we would exit the planet once our work was done, we being in this case an extended soul group. Ophiuchus was the place where we'd be able to access a portal, the thirteenth master sign.

The problem with the story of the thirteen crystal skulls is that there are more than thirteen ancient crystal skulls. There doesn't seem to be one original set of thirteen that has been identified as The Ones. Stephen thinks there are sets of thirteen in different areas. We both feel Max was one of a set of thirteen. Once he told me he held the matrix for the planet. He didn't share the details. I doubt I had the bandwidth at that time to take it in. Einstein, however, has the energy and intelligence to sit in the middle of any circle of ancient skulls. He feels like a master skull.

On 11-11-11, Kendall moved his conference to L.A. There we met even more skulls and were surrounded by crystal dealers selling many contemporary pieces. An antiquities dealer came by and showed us a piece he said had been cursed. One of Stephen's old friends, who was a strong psychic, did some work to clear it.

The secret reveal at this conference was Ixchel, a skull named for the Mayan moon and fertility goddess. The keeper had another skull with her that was carved with a monkey face. I didn't catch its name, but I found myself thinking of him as her companion skull, much like a high-strung racehorse needs a pony or donkey in its stall to help him stay calm. Ixchel was just like that—high-strung. She seemed somewhat distraught to me. When two men in the group with the Mayan Daykeepers came and sang to her, she settled right down. Ixchel is a powerful skull, but I wasn't able to really sync with her. Skulls are like meditation techniques in that humans resonate with different ones. I liken it to radio stations back in the day. We'd move the dial until we found the station that was broadcasting the music we liked. In terms of skulls and meditation, it's a question of resonance, which frequency we resonate with.

My favorite skull will always be Max. He shot me into Christ Consciousness for a day and introduced me to Stephen. After that event in Boulder, Stephen and I started hosting Max at our house. We even slept with him next to the bed. Max offered relationship advice, even once explained to Stephen what to cook for lunch and how to serve it to everyone while we were hosting visitors to meditate with Max. He always dispensed spiritual energy and unconditional love. Once he said to Stephen, "So I put you two together to work. What have you done?" It was like he was expecting a progress report.

A few years back, we traveled to Sedona to stay with Stephen's publisher, David Hatcher Childress, and tootle around the ancient sites and fun stores in town. We also visited with Einstein. In the middle of working with Einstein, Caroline turned to me and said that the relationships crystal skulls arrange should not be judged by ordinary standards. She said something like, "We don't look like normal couples." Here she pointed to her own partner. "The skulls want us to do our work. We're here to uplift the world. It's not a Harlequin romance."

How did this second awakening change me? Max gave me the strength to do a lot of the spiritual work for the world that was part of my agreement for this life. Before Max introduced us, Stephen had been to Egypt one time. Now he's been twenty-two times and led twenty tours. He'd published a few articles before. Now he has three books out, two on Egypt and another on crystal skulls. Before Max put us together, I'd written one novel. It was unpublished. Now, I have nine novels published, and also a handful of short stories. I've been to Egypt four times. We've also traveled together to England, Scotland, and Peru with him being a speaker on tours. I've gone on trips to Cambodia and the south of France on my own. I was also changed internally. I continued to grow spiritually, with deeper experiences in mediation, and with guidance and intuition.

The last time I saw Max, I'd had some neck surgery. He directed the whole group to work on our fifth chakra. I felt a good amount of healing then. Max will always be a part of our lives. Stephen asked just the other day if a crystal person we know in southern Colorado would be hosting Max again soon. Our current house is just too small. It would be nice to see our old friend again. I'm sure we will.

When I first saw Max, he asked me not to take a picture of him. "The next time this energy comes to you, it will be in a different form." He didn't want me to get attached to him in particular as the source of enlightenment. This does not explain how many contemporary crystal skulls we have in our house, of course. Humans will be humans. We collect images or items that remind us of our spiritual portals. Sometimes we start to mistake those images or items with the spiritual experience, which is what Max was warning me about. The founder of Zen, Wu Hsin, talks about it as worshiping the signpost to spiritual growth rather than proceeding along the path (although he doesn't believe in a 'path', but never mind about that). All our skulls have been around Max and I carry a palm-sized one with me to conferences and sacred sites to gather energy and bring it home.

But Max was right about this consciousness coming to me from a different source the next time. It happened at a sacred site in the South of France and once again took me completely by surprise.

SACRED SITES

7

THE THIRD TIME I EXPERIENCED samadhi, I was leaning against the tower of a fourteenth-century Cathar castle in the Aude département in the South of France, gazing out at the mountains where many famous villages nestle. The year was 2021.

It happened on almost the last day of the Mary Magdalene tour I was on. As I sat listening to our tour guide talk about this site, an energy started building around the corner of the tower. Finally, it was so intense that I left the group to see what it was. I leaned against the ancient stone wall and looked out at the valley with the blue mountains rising in the distance. The mountains seemed to be cradling a sacred heart. I caught my breath at the beauty of it. The energy opened up, rushing in to fill me, and I was thrown into an exalted state of consciousness. How can I describe it? Hafiz says it best: "Love popped the cork on itself — splattered my brains across the sky" (lines 5-9).[12] That is exactly what happened.

Sacred spots, power places, can hold the untainted energy of pure consciousness and transmit it to us. They can give us access to enlightenment. I have not named the place where I had this experience, not out of a desire to hide it from you, but because power places are just like meditation techniques or crystal skulls or any other doorway to enlightenment. We each find the one that resonates with us.

This happens in Egypt. As we travel the Nile and go to many of the temples on her banks, people are eager to have direct spiritual experiences. Inevitably, most people find their special spot. They walk away from the temple, their eyes the size of saucers or their faces streaming with tears of joy. Then we'd go to the next temple, all built on sacred sites, and another person would say, "Oh my God! You won't believe what happened!" Actually, we could believe it, but the point is not everyone gets lit up by the same spot. We all resonate with different energies. Not each and every single person is unique to one spot. Maybe we have energetic tribes, groups that are affected by one site, one meditation, one crystal rather than another one. I am certain, though, there is a spot, a technique, for each and every one of us.

I remember being at one of the crystal skull conferences in Sedona and an indigenous presenter had brought a set of flutes. When played, they weren't harmonious in the traditional way we think of in western music, but they set up a resonant field in which each person was supposed to hear their own special body note. I remember listening to them and hearing a note that wasn't exactly what was being played. Was this my body note? Then someone in the aisle behind me hummed what they were hearing. It was most

---

[12] Hafiz. "I Imagine Now for Ages," *The Gift*. Translated by Daniel Ladinsky, Penguin, 1999, 209.

decidedly not what I was hearing. This was her note. I had my own.

People have recognized power spots for thousands of years. In Egypt, you can find layers of buildings in the same place. This is not done for convenience, but because the energy of area is special. Scratch the ground of a mosque, church or synagogue there, and you're likely to find the ceiling of another building. In Luxor Temple, the top of a column was discovered poking up through the sand. Of course there was another temple underneath the current one. Rather than excavate, the authorities decided to just cover it up again. Thousands of people visit this beautiful temple. An excavation could take years and tourists would not be able to visit the site. People would lose their experience. Egypt would lose money. Egyptians depend on tourism for their livelihood.

Stephen's archaeological background shows when he explains the sites in Egypt. "On top is the current Muslim layer. Peel that back and you find the Coptic Christian layer, then the Roman layer, then Jewish, then Greek, then dynastic, and finally pre-dynastic."

The same is true in France. A small chapel named St Salvyre perches high in the mountains above the town of Alet-les-Bains. Dedicated to Mary Magdalene by the locals, it now serves as a place for deep meditation. The altar sits in the center of the structure with four arms coming off forming a Celtic Cross. This chapel is built on an ancient Mithras Temple. And before that? Who knows, but a natural vortex rises from the earth here. The energy drops into the earth, then rises up and spreads, forming a sphere of energy. This chapel would have knocked my socks off if I hadn't already been blasted into orbit earlier in the day. This sacred place allowed me to slowly assimilate the energy from the experience I mentioned above.

Alet-les-Bains is called the Chosen Place. The most recent explanation for this name is that a viscount of Razés built an abbey there that became the bishop's seat. Huguenots destroyed the abbey in the sixteenth century, probably in retribution for the war against the Cathars. According to the local teachers, many Cathars became Huguenots to hide from the crusade against them.

In the early 1500's, Nostradamus spent part of his childhood here. The town had a strong Jewish community, contributing their knowledge of the Kabbalah to what was surely an already thriving spiritual center. You can see Stars of David in the church in town. The abbey may have been built on a temple to Diana just like many churches in France. Alet-les-Bains was a chosen place well before Christianity even existed.

Home of Nostradamus in Alet-les-Bains
Photo by Theresa Crater

How about the famous town of Rennes-le-Château? Built on a Temple to Isis, it's under the park at the top of the hill next to Bérenger Saunière's famous tower. To the best of my knowledge, the Isis tradition is still continuing with a priestess of Isis presiding over the town today. The contemporary Templar Order also has a headquarters here.

Bérenger Saunière's tower in Rennes-le-Château
Photo by Theresa Crater

What makes a power spot? In Egypt, Hakim said underground streams, crystals in the earth, and the sun combined to create special energetics in places. The water runs through crystalline rock, generating energy, and in Egypt, holes in the tunnels let the sunlight beam in, adding more energy. This theory holds for Alet. The town is full of springs. The mountains are full of rocks with crystalline structures embedded in them. The water is still safe to drink. I'd say it's beyond safe. It's full of natural minerals and charged with energy. One ninety-year-old man we met there looked to be in his sixties.

Some people theorize the earth has dragon or ley lines just like the human body has meridians. These lines carry more energy than other areas around them. The well-known Michael and Mary lines run through Europe. Some claim they run farther, up from the Middle East. Cathedrals, chapels, wells can be found on these lines. Some of the monasteries built on the Michael line run from Skellig Michael in Ireland all the way to Santuario di San Michele del Gargano in Italy, and it includes famous sites such as St Michael's Mount in Cornwall (UK), Mont Saint-Michel in Normandy (France), the Island of Delos (Greece), Symi (Greece), Kourion (Cyprus), and Mount Carmel (Israel).

The Mary Michael Pilgrim's Way in the south of England includes famous power spots as well as ones that are not so well known. St Michael's Mount, Glastonbury Tor, and the Avebury complex are among the better known. Other sites were probably better known years in the past, like the South Zeal Menhir stone which aids in fertility. [13]

Peru has its own set of energy lines. The Coricancha, the Golden Enclosure in Cousco, once held the Incan Temples of the Sun and Moon. Now a cathedral stands next to it, sharing part of the same spot of the ancient temples. From the center of the courtyard in the Coricancha, forty-two energy lines or *seques* radiate out. Each one runs to a sacred place or *huaca*. These are either naturally occurring sites, like springs, caves, special boulders, or man-made buildings, canals, or fountains. From above, the temple resembled the sun with the rays running out in all directions.

---

[13] Visit https://britishpilgrimage.org/portfolio/mary-and-michael-pilgrims-way/ for the full list.

The first time I remember the land speaking to me was in the Appalachian mountains of North Carolina. This was around 1972. I was attending a TM residence course, a weekend retreat for extended meditation and lectures. These courses usually started with a group meditation, and there were thirty of us at least, probably more.

About halfway into the meditation, the mountain woke up. It's like it stirred in its sleep and open its eyes. I heard it say, "I haven't felt this in a very long time." The mountain was pleased. I felt as if it had announced some kind of turning point, like perhaps we were headed once again toward that time it remembered, when people gathered consciously to meditate, raise their frequency, tune to their surroundings, grow toward enlightenment.

There is nothing special about this particular mountain that I am aware of. No legends are associated with it. It's not a famous place that people visit. Somebody told me Billy Graham's house was on the other side of the mountain, but I don't think that makes this place a power spot. The mountain did wake up to appreciate our collective meditation.

The second time the land spoke to me was a few decades later when I first visited England. It was 1990. My mother's ancestry is mostly English and Dutch. I've always been drawn to the Arthurian legends. I was teaching British literature at the time. Did this for close to thirty years. Perhaps all this combined to call me to England. When I first stepped foot on the ground there, it greeted me. It was like it said hello, like it recognized me. A part of me belonged there. Perhaps I'd returned home.

That summer we tootled around London, went to Oxford, saw a Shakespeare play in Stratford-upon-Avon, saw his home, then visited Stonehenge. At last, a famous power spot. From the road, Stonehenge looked smaller than I expected. Just like the Sphinx looked smaller. We parked and walked toward the circle. As I got closer, the atmosphere of the place crept up on me. Ominous. Not joyful as I expected. I've learned since from another visit and from other people that this place is moody. It can be brimming with light or gloomy like English clouds. That day it was broody. It mumbled to me, grumbled, filled me with a sense of unease. I was inexperienced. I didn't know what I was feeling or what to do with the energy. I was traveling with somebody who didn't really believe in my psychic ability. That can make a big difference, especially when you're just developing your capacity to attune to these places.

Me in "Devil's Seat" in Avebury
Photo by Ruth Adele

We also visited Avebury, and here the power of the stones—being able to go up to them and touch them—made my experience more palpable. I sat in what was dubbed as the Devil's Seat and felt a hug. A few years later, I returned to Avebury by myself. A stone just off the road near the Red Lion pub had scaffolding surrounding it. Some work was being done here. I sat under this stone and leaned against it to meditate. After about a minute, the stone asked, "Aren't you afraid I'm going to topple over on you?"

I jumped up. Was this the reason the stone had been shored up with a scaffold? The stone was surprised by my reaction. First, that I'd heard its thoughts. Second, that I'd taken it seriously. It seemed a bit chagrined. We sort of chuckled together and I sat back down, meditating for some more time. Nothing much came to me. Just the feel of wind, the tickle of sheep's teeth nibbling grass.

I've always felt this was an important circle, but it's taken a lot of damage. In the early days of Christianity in Britain, some say the Druids and Christian monks lived in harmony. But this changed as Celtic Christianity gave way to Roman Catholicism, which was at the time more hostile toward other spiritualities. (Some claim there was always hostility.) The church taught these stone circles were used for devil worship. Many stones in the Avebury circle were buried, pulled down, or even hacked apart because of these teachings. It wasn't until the 1930s that Alexander Keiller bought the site and began restoration. Perhaps this damage lessened its ability to talk to us, but I somehow doubt this. I think this circle isn't a strong signal for me, as much as I'd like it to be. It doesn't exactly match my resonance frequency as strongly as some other places do. I still love it, though.

The Tor and the twin springs in Glastonbury hold a special place in my heart. When I walked on the ridge of Wearyall Hill, I had a brief glimpse into the past of the water and green hills rising up from the mists. I've visited other circles in England and Scotland, crawled into Maeshowe and other cairns, and caught little glimpses of life in the past. None of them have blasted me into a higher state of consciousness, but they might do that to you.

In 1997, I traveled to the big island of Hawai'i and Pele spoke to me directly. Pele is the goddess of fire and volcanoes, known as *Pelehonuamea*, "she who shapes the sacred land" of *ka wahine ai honua*, "the woman who devours the land." Many legends surround her. Someone will pick up a lone woman hitchhiking along the roads on the big island. She gets in the back seat. The person drives for a while, turns to speak with her, and there's nobody there. Some say she especially lures men into the lava flows. If her lava is flowing toward your dwelling, locals recommend propitiating her with gin.

As soon as I stepped off the plane in Hawai'i, I felt the island connect with me. It was a warm energy under my feet. One day I was hiking with a friend, another skeptic. This doubt disturbs our experience of sacred places, although I didn't realize how much at the time. We went into one of the national parks. I'd been studying

Native American traditions for a little while. My teacher was part Cheyenne, but had been trained by a Hopi man. I wanted to make a medicine wheel, so we hiked into a rocky area and I gathered stones, asking their permission, and started to make the wheel. My friend sat off and watched, and I could feel her doubt. I also knew she didn't approve of me using sage as an offering. After I finished the wheel and told her I felt her disapproval, she said she wondered if I was introducing a foreign plant into the ecosystem. But that wasn't the end of it. She said she hadn't felt anything.

I did, though. Pele talked to me in the middle of the ceremony. She greeted and encouraged me. I don't remember all the details, but what stuck with me was that there was talk that Pele would only speak to indigenous Hawaiians, but here she was communicating with me. I asked her why. She pointed out how I'd always lived near mountains—in the foothills of the Appalachian chain, in view of Mt. Rainier, how I'd often done my TM training courses in the Alps. That's when she said, *You're not named* Crater *for nothing*. This made me laugh. I felt like a part of her family. Extended family, for sure, but like I'd been accepted by a powerful spiritual protector of an important place.

The volcanoes of Hawai'i are indeed powerful. We went down to another part of the national park where the lava was erupting and falling into the sea. As I watched this amazingly powerful process, I felt the land telling me how it forms continents. It's easy to believe considering many kinds of ecosystems exist on the big island—deserts, tropical forests, grasslands, mountains. Everything you find around the globe. The islands of Hawai'i were created by Kīlauea. As I understand it, the Pacific Mantle moves northwest away from the Hawaiian hot spot, resulting in the chain of islands. It's a slow process, although eruptions aren't always slow. The awe from standing next to the lava erupting into the sea can't be overstated. Perhaps the power of Hawai'i helped me be open to the experience I had with Max.

The geysers of Yellowstone have a similar effect. There's something about witnessing the raw power of the earth's volcanoes that puts me in touch with deep, primal energy. But Yellowstone didn't talk to me. I loved it and felt the sacredness of the place—nature left intact with her creatures. But Yellowstone does talk to other people. I know this because of a man in our campgrounds who exuded to me. "I'm in Yellowstone," he said, his eyes dancing. "Yellowstone! Anything could happen." It was clear to me that this was his spot.

I lived in Seattle when Mount Saint Helens erupted. She didn't warn me or talk to me, either. I remember sitting at my dining room table one early spring evening before the big eruption. I'd just laid out an I-Ching reading and received a changing hexagram. I don't remember the original one, but when I opened the book to read about the new hexagram and saw the title Critical Mass, the whole room rocked gently back and forth. I looked up and saw a cut-glass suncatcher hanging in the window swinging back and forth. Everything settled down after about ten seconds. I was impressed! An earthquake during a divination. That was a sign, I thought, although I don't remember what the question was now.

The next morning standing in line at the bank, the conversations were comical. A woman whispered to her friend, "We were in bed—you know." Her friend nodded, understanding the unspoken. "It was just—" she waved her hand in the air "—amazing. I said, 'I think the earth moved.' He said, 'It did. I think there was an earthquake.'"

Her friend laughed loudly, then covered her mouth, although everyone around them was smiling, obviously listening in. "I didn't realize he meant like there really was an earthquake."

I overhear another conversation. "My friend's in a crisis. She was praying. She said out loud, 'Please, give me a sign.' Then the earthquake hit."

"Oh, my," the other person said.

A few days later, Mount Saint Helens blew her top. I realized I'd been tense and cranky for a couple of days. That all released when the mountain exploded. We were lucky in Seattle that the ash and debris mostly blew east. I noticed a light dusting on the surfaces outside, but nothing significant. Several smaller quakes followed the eruption. I noticed I would get headaches for a day or few hours before the quakes would hit, and afterwards they'd immediately dissipate. The TM movement still had my phone number somehow and they called me. They wanted to have a group meditation to "alleviate the effects of Mt. Saint Helens." At the time, I thought this was the height of hubris. Who were we to interfere with such titanic forces? I thought that the earth knew what she was doing.

Animals sense coming quakes. Birds take to the sky in huge flocks. The wild animals flee well before the danger strikes. We humans have been trained out of our awareness of such things. All life is all tuned to the land in ways we do not understand.

8

I'VE ALREADY WRITTEN ABOUT THE Sphinx talking to me when I first arrived in Egypt. This ancient land has a series of power spots that runs up the Nile. Some of the oases are energetically powerful as well, but I haven't visited them.

Each time I've gone to the Isis Temple on Agilkia Island, I enjoy myself looking at the glyphs, meditating in the Holy of Holies, playing with the cats at the café. But the real vision came to me on Bigeh. When the dam was built, much of the area around Aswan flooded. The Isis Temple had to be moved from its original site on the island of Bigeh to Agilkia. Hakim took us to Bigeh. We picked our way over an ancient jetty to a damp area. The island had recently flooded. Hakim invited us to find places to sit for our meditation. I leaned up against a fallen log.

I don't remember Hakim's meditation because the priestesses of Isis came for me immediately. I remember being dressed in a flowing, diaphanous robe and led to an altar. The priestesses removed my robe and helped me lie down on the stone altar. They circled me and chanted. A priest arrived dressed in some special way. I couldn't quite see how because his erect phallus got my attention. We performed the sacred marriage on the altar. As we finished, I heard Hakim calling us out of the meditation. He gave me a significant nod as if to say *well done.*

Hakim teaching me on the Giza Plateau
Photo by Rob Arlinghaus

One of my favorite sacred spots along the Nile is the Temple of Kom Ombo, dedicated to the crocodile Neter Sobek and the hawk Horus, the son of Isis and Osiris. My experience of Sobek is that he rules the spine. When a crocodile walks, its spine and tail moves in a flowing motion. At this temple, we got to experience this personally.

Sobek is also known as the great digester. According to my Egyptian friends, he especially digests anger. At the time, I was stuck in a dysfunctional job and I have to admit I'd gotten chronically angry. My early spiritual training had led me to expect

I could manifest my desires. I shouldn't be stuck. I'd been meditating for close to thirty years at this point. What was wrong with me? I applied for jobs and got interviews, but no offers. In truth, I think I'd passed the magical age barrier. Earlier in life, it seemed I could point at a job and it was mine. Now nothing panned out. My disillusionment probably showed. Maybe the sparkle had worn off. Maybe this was why I didn't get any offers. My Egyptian friends recognized my anger and kept giving me statues of Sobek.

"He will help you," they said.

On my first visit to Kom Ombo, Hakim showed us the glyphs of medical instruments toward the back of the temple. Then the hole in the wall with the ear where the priests were said to eavesdrop on the people coming into the temple. Next we moved to the side wall and he talked about the images of the forty-two tribes of ancient Khemit. Finally, he took us to the initiation spot. Stephen called this the Fear Initiation. In the past, this area was filled with water—and crocodiles. The initiate had to dive into this pool of water and swim through a very tight channel at the bottom with the crocodiles looking on. No problem, right? What they weren't told was that the crocodiles had been fed and were mostly lazing in the sun.

Hakim took us one by one into a little nook in front of the tunnel and recited a Khemitian prayer. At the end of this, he turned each one of us around and said, "There is nothing to fear." He led us to a grate covering the tunnel, opened it, and we crawled in. I scrambled on all fours for a few feet, but then it got even tighter and I was forced to drop down on my belly. That's when I tuned into the rhythm of a reptile—one arm and the opposite leg moving forward, then the other arm and leg, with the spine undulating as I moved. I even had the sensation of having a tail.

Then something hit me. A huge fist of energy slammed down on top of me. I suppose this was the power spot of the temple. The sheer force of it could freak a person out! For me, the feel of a crocodile overtook me. I scurried forward, filled with the joy of movement, brimming with the primal dynamism of life. I was all spine. I reached the end of the tunnel in another few feet and crawled up to the people waiting to receive me in my rebirth. I meeped like a baby crocodile. Stephen fell out laughing.

Unfortunately, the grates are now firmly locked. I suppose with enough baksheesh, you could talk a keeper into unlocking them and repeat this initiation for yourself. Once I told another person who had traveled a few times to Egypt what my favorite spots were. "Really, the most powerful experiences have been in Kom Ombo and the Sekhmet shrine in Karnack."

"You are a dark goddess," was her appraisal. Both of these Neters—Sobek and Sekhmet—yield a lot of power and can be intimidating.

The most powerful experience I had in Egypt was at Karnak. After walking through the entryway of the huge complex, Hakim steered us off to the left. I was grateful when he said, "We shall approach the Holy of Holies in silence."

The group followed behind him like a row of ducklings.

As we walked, I gazed up at the obelisks rising behind the rows of columns, all deeply engraved with various glyphs I couldn't make out yet. Leaving the more even paths most tourists follow, we walked across a span of sand and rock. I glanced down to be careful of my footing, and when I raised my eyes again, I saw a woman walking toward me from the temple, dressed in long flowing robes and carrying a basket of flowers.

"Welcome home," she said. I looked into the woman's face and recognized—myself. Suddenly, the temple walls blossomed with color, the trees leafed in an instant, and the sand turned green beneath my now-sandaled feet. Around a corner, the scent of flowers from a verdant garden filled the air. Water splashed in a fountain and a woman sitting on a bench looked up at me and smiled.

Our group in the present moment was joined by a long procession of men and women from the past, all carrying baskets overflowing with red, yellow, pink, and blue blossoms, all chanting in a complex harmony that pebbled my flesh. Brilliantly colored birds flew among us and perched in the trees, adding their song. The chant was but one part of the deep harmony, the

132

complete openness of one heart to another, the perfect accord of that community of many who were one.

Tears flowed unchecked down my face as I walked in both times, reliving the age when we had all lived in full consciousness, open to the singing birds, the shining faces of the flowers, the majestic river slowly winding through the land, the sun beaming down on his earth, the galaxies swinging in great spirals, and all life, here and in the higher frequencies, creating a great symphony of oneness.

In the present, an antiquities guard rushed toward me, concerned I was crying. Hakim shooed him away, for which I will be eternally grateful. We made our way through a corridor formed by smaller stone columns, a soft dun in the present-day sun, leaping with color in the past. We approached a sanctuary.

Stephen had told me where we were going when we were still on the boat, but I'd forgotten. Egypt can be overwhelming with its abundance of sites and I prefer to be surprised. This leaves me open to whatever energy presents itself. Hakim allowed each person to go in alone. I passed the flat, dusty altar outside the shrine, went through an entry room and into the chamber on the right.

There she stood beneath a pinprick in the limestone ceiling illuminating her face, the Neter Sekhmet. But I did not see the statue. I saw the Neter herself, gazing down through layers of space and time, a look of deep compassion on her face. She understood how difficult it is to live in this time. She reached out to me with pure love.

My knees buckled. I fell at the great one's feet and wept. From me poured all the pain of separation I'd ever felt in this life. The perfect peace of the past filled me and covered the cuts and bruises like a golden unguent, healing in an instant all the aches, all the fears, all the yearnings for what I could never name until now.

Stand up, dear one.

Sekhmet's voice was a golden bell in my mind. I rose and placed a small crystal on the flat top of the lotus staff that ended just under the goddess's breasts, in the fierce heart of the great lioness.

Take my hands.

I placed my flesh hands over the stone hands of the Neter and closed my eyes. From somewhere far above, an enormous river of light flooded the chamber. I felt as if I was standing in a column of honey, thick and golden, vibrating with the voices of a thousand bees. When time began again, Sekhmet spoke her blessing, telling me she would always be with me.

I didn't experience Unity during this time. Perhaps my mind was caught up in the vision of the past, but the healing I experienced was complete, at least for a while. Hakim kept an eye on me during the rest of our visit. I walked in silence, filled with peace. It was difficult to take in any information about the large Karnak site, but I live with an encyclopedia about Egypt and need only ask any time.

Hundreds of people have had extraordinary experiences in this little chapel on the far side of Karnack. I've seen people burst into tears, stand shaking their heads in disbelief, talk about hearing her voice. When my friends who still lead tours post a picture of her in her sanctuary, many people will comment on how much they love her, how special she is, how they were astonished by their experience with her and return to her whenever they visit Egypt.

Sekhmet
Photo by Stephen Mehler

Sekhmet is usually depicted as a warrior goddess. The story is that Ra enlisted her to destroy humans because they were not worshiping the gods and goddesses. Shades of the flood story. The Hopi have a similar one. In response to Ra's request, Sekhmet went on a killing rampage, drinking the blood of the dead and dying. The only way Ra could stop her was to give her pomegranate wine, which she drank until she passed out. When she woke, she had supposedly returned to her benign form, her "twin" Neter Hathor.

Stephen and I believe this is a patriarchal myth. Sekhmet is the pure love of Mother. She is also The Power, the Unconditional Love of Mother. When we stand in front of her, she will confront us if we are out of alignment. She doesn't do this in any mean way. She simply points out the imbalance and, in my experience, gives us about three seconds to respond. Any resistance or denial will be met with a slap upside the head with her paw. Metaphorically speaking, of course.

Stephen said he met the disciplinarian when he first stood in front of her. She pointed out something she was not happy with; he never told me what it was and I don't need to know. It's between them. Stephen said he fell to his knees before her, giving up this imbalance when face to face with her. She forgave her son instantly.

To fathom this implacable side of her, it's helpful to explore her place on the Kabalistic Tree of Life. Sekhmet stands on the path from Tiphareth to Geburah. Forgive me for going 'all nerdy' on you for a minute. You can skip it if you're not up for a quick lesson on Kabbalah.

Tiphareth is in the middle of the tree, the sphere of the sacrificed god. This is the sphere of Christ Consciousness. I was happy to discover this after my experience with Max. Geburah is above this heart center on the right shoulder. On the left shoulder is Chesed. (This is when you've stepped into the tree. When you are facing it, it's the opposite.) In the Lord's Prayer, these two spheres are referred to as "the power and the glory." The pharaoh holds two implements representing them in his hands—the crook in his left hand, the flail in his right.

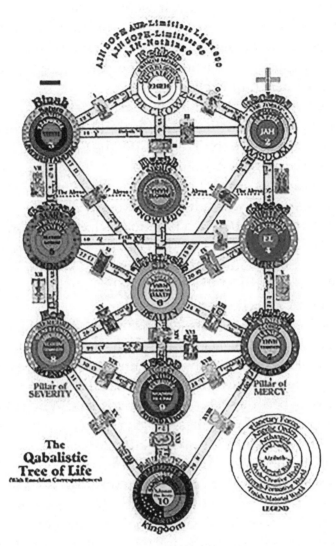

Tree of Life
(VendettaXIII, 2019) CC BY 4.0

These qualities must be in balance in a person, in a ruler, in the world. Too much mercy leads to weakness. At some point, you must stand up to the bully, discipline the miscreant. The vice of Chesed is traditionally tyranny, but observing the world today, it seems apparent to me it is also weakness—giving mercy to those who are taking advantage of a soft heart. The vice of Geburah is cruelty, going too far with discipline and harming the person rather than creating a way for her/him to change.

We can understand the relationship between these two by thinking about how the universe manifests from the One Consciousness. On the Tree of Life, the One is the top sphere, Kether, the Absolute, wants to know itself and in order to do this, it must manifest. It sends out energy which manifests as the next sphere, Chokmah. One image associated with Chokmah is a mirror. In the mirror, Kether sees itself so to speak. Let's just say the sight is impressive. Chokmah flows out and creates the third sphere, Binah. Binah is the Great Mother, who begins to create form. The creation process begins.

The Vedas describe the exact same process all packed into the word 'satchitananda.' They say the Absolute or 'sat,' which is pure being or the quantum state if you're into physics, becomes aware of itself. The Absolute becomes conscious, becomes 'chit' or consciousness. When Being experiences itself, becomes conscious of itself, it explodes in bliss. This wave of joy is the creation, or *ananda*.

Back to the Tree of Life. After Binah comes Chesed. Yes, fellow mystics, I'm skipping Daath for now. It's a hidden sphere anyway, right? Chesed takes the forms and sends them to Geburah. It's Geburah's job to determine if the ideas Chesed sends are actually practical. Will they work in the manifest world? Will they hold up? If so, great. The energy flows down the tree. If not, she—Geburah is considered female—says no and stops the idea from manifesting.

Remember how I wrote that eastern traditions start the spiritual journey by aiming for the top—for Pure

Consciousness. We transcend more and more, and this clears us up—eventually. Some western traditions seem to do the opposite. We start at the bottom of the Tree of Life when we use it as a tool for meditation and work our way up to the top. This clears us up—eventually.

So, Sekhmet stands on the path between Geburah to Tiphareth, the sphere next on the tree. What does this mean? Moving up from Tiphareth into Geburah, the energy is so high that we must be in perfect balance to withstand it. Simple as that. Any imbalance will throw our form into disarray and we will slide back down the tree. Sekhmet enforces this. She doesn't want us to be destroyed by the high frequency, so she points out our imbalances.

Okay, that took longer to explain than I expected. Sekhmet as disciplinarian is not the main experience of being with her. It's not something many people talk about after they've seen her. They mostly mention her all-encompassing love. Stephen says she embodies the love of Mother. She brought me into harmony, showed me a past I remember with gratitude and joy, and blessed me in the present. She still does.

What about this dual time experience? It is said that everything that happens in a place leaves an impression. A permanent impression. Some traditions talk about the Akashic Records, an ethereal area close to pure consciousness where a record of all events are stored. I think I saw my past when I was a priestess of Sekhmet.

I'm not the only person who's had dual-time experiences in Egypt. I spoke with a woman who had a special affinity with Abydos, home of the Osirion. A beautiful corridor stretches inside this temple. She was walking down this corridor, feeling grateful to be back in her spiritual home. Suddenly she realized that if she took one more step, she would be transported back in time. She stopped, contemplating if she wanted to leave this life and return to ancient Egypt.

"It was a difficult choice," she said, "but I decided to stay."

Are there such things as time portals? Entrances into other dimensions and places? Well, they certainly show up in science fiction and fantasy. Maybe there are some that actually exist. On my trip to Egypt in 2013, we got to visit the Serapeum. This is an underground structure with a corridor filled with niches holding many huge diorite boxes. Diorite is often called black granite and is high in silicate minerals. It's said these are sarcophagi used to bury the Apis bull, the most important bull deity of ancient Egypt.

Me in the Serapeum
Photo by Patricia Awyan

Let's just say I think this is bunk, and many other people do, too. Maybe centuries after they were built when their original use had been forgotten people used them for this purpose. But why make tombs for bulls so perfect? The tolerances on the inside of these boxes are up to one-tenth of a human hair. That means the variances in the surface is microscopic. It is space-age even. Smoother than a baby's — well, you know.

We walked down steps and then down some more, and arrived in the underground facility. We turned next to a large box and walked down to a corridor filled with niches. I went to the first one. That's when the visions began. I began to see keepers in each niche who seemed to be in charge of operating the box in that space. What were they for? This began to unfold to me as I continued down the hallway.

I wish I could go through it niche by niche and describe every world and every operator, but I can't remember it that clearly. I saw attendants in mostly every niche. Behind them, the walls began to shimmer and display pictures. These pictures started to come alive, showing different worlds. Real worlds. Worlds to be visited through these niches somehow.

Through the windows that formed on the wall were images, colors, and feelings of the world that niche connected to. The attendants reached out and touched me with their scepters. Some on the third eye, some on the shoulder. Some acknowledged me with a simple nod. Others made hand gestures or waved for me to come into a niche.

The gigantic stone boxes were filled with liquid light. That's the only way to describe it. I realized they were transport devices to other worlds. I asked how they worked, and the third or so guardian told me, "They work much like the crystal you described in your book." He was referring to the first two books in the Power Places series, *Under the Stone Paw* and *Beneath the Hallowed Hill*. In these books, giant crystal were used to "beam" to other places and times. In the Serapeum, the person would lay in the box and be transported to the place specific to that niche. Just sort of dissolved into energy. In other niches, I saw people turning into Neters.

The 'window' walls showed solar worlds, filled with light and gold and sun. Others had many colors. Some were night worlds. These began toward the end of the corridor and mostly on the left side. Some were very green and filled with plants. Others desert and sand. Some were water worlds. In one of the night worlds, the guardian came forward to greet me and a big black jaguar joined him and licked my face.

There were twenty-seven boxes in the hallway. Then I went down the hallway that intersected them, shaped sort of like an H, but not with even arms. There were some unfinished niches on that side. Stephen went further and said there was a workshop in the back. He says there's a door blocking another tunnel and there are more niches—who knows how many.

I went back and counted them. Twenty-seven. At first, I counted the box without a lid next to the door. If there are more, I'm curious how they are grouped. In certain numbers? I'd like to go there with a master toner and see what happens. One of the women I traveled with is married to an engineer who has studied Egypt extensively. He was a speaker on the tour. She had a dream about the Serapeum. It matched almost exactly what I'd seen. I had not discussed my vision with her. After we talked, she suggested the next time we go, each of us should sit in one of the boxes and tone. Truth be told, I'm not sure I have the nerve to do that, just like my friend who did not take the next step in Abydos to a different time or the time I didn't go explore the UFO hovering right next to the freeway.

When we left the Serapeum, one of the tour members had gone out early and was waiting for the group. She walked up to me and said, "When you've seen one box, you've seen them all." A Neter-like being, at least seven feet tall if not more, had walked out with me. I had her on one side, him on the other. I marveled at the contrast. We all resonate with different places.

The vendors awaited us. The Egyptian revolution had seriously cut into their business, so they were eager for us to ride their camels or donkeys. One said to us, "Five dollars American," and I completely cracked up, imagining if this Neter were fully present in our dimension, he would look at some chronometer on his wrist and think, *Blast, I'm in the wrong century*.

When I was in the Serapeum, I thought I was seeing other worlds, other planets that make up our stellar family. But then I thought they were possibly dimensions. Perhaps it's not a matter of time—that in the distant past we used this place in this way—but a matter of layers, that in some higher frequency we still use this place as a transportation and healing nexus.

While visiting the Angkor temples in Cambodia, I had one other interdimensional experience. The year was 2017. On the first full day, we visited the Angkor Wat temple. After exploring on my own for a while, I joined the group as the guide explained the sculpted bas-relief called the Churning of the Ocean of Milk. Taking up forty-nine meters on the side of the temple, the sculpture depicts the famous Hindu story from the Mahabharata when the *devas* (gods) and *asuras* (demons) churn the primordial ocean (Binah, by the way, in the Kabalistic tradition) to create *amrita*, the elixir of immortality. Note that the positive and negative charges of creation are needed to accomplish this feat.

Bridge to Angkor Thom ~ This bridge shows positive and negative "charges" with devas on one side and rakshasas on the other.
Photo by Theresa Crater

After admiring the bas-relief, the rest of the tour group started climbing to the higher levels of the temple—five levels representing the holy mountain, Meru. I was having trouble with my hip, so I decided to sit down between the statues of various Hindu and Buddhist divinities and teachers, decapitated by the Khmer Rouge when they made the temple their headquarters between 1975-79. I nestled between two unidentifiable gods in a narrow hallway and meditated.

After maybe ten or fifteen minutes, I began to see in my inner vision that the top of the temple seemed to be undulating. I settled deeper, hoping to see more clearly. Visions are like cats. They come to you. Reaching and trying simply drive them farther away—just like pure consciousness in meditation. Frustrating for us Westerners who are taught that working hard, making strenuous effort, is the way to success.

After some more time, I saw that the undulation was a deity who sat atop the temple in a higher dimension. He rolled around, swaying his body and head in a sort of circle, waving his many arms. I couldn't see clearly enough to count them. The temple was dedicated to the triad of Hindu gods—Shiva, Vishnu, and Brahma—but it seemed to me that this deity was Vishnu himself. This was one of those times when I only saw pictures in my head. I didn't connect emotionally or spiritually with the Divine One, but I knew he was there, still active, still blessing everyone and all that lay around with his movements motivated by the bliss of creation.

I enjoyed the temples of Angkor, returning to my Vedic teachings and seeing them displayed on the walls, but I didn't make any more psychic connections or have any experiences of higher states of consciousness while there. Maybe it was the humidity. Even in winter, this is a land of at least two showers a day.

9

MY THIRD SAMADHI HAPPENED IN France. I'd been getting an urge to explore the South of France for several years. I went so far as to develop an itinerary for a Templar tour, but Stephen didn't get excited enough about it for us to implement it. After the COVID crisis calmed down in the summer of 2021, I decided it was safe enough to travel. I guess I had cabin fever. I explored the available tours, wanting to go with a guide who really knew the area.

I found Veronique Flayol online, a native of St Maximin la Sainte Baume and founder of Magdalene Sacred Journeys. She responded to my email inquiry, telling me she had to cancel the summer tour that fit my teaching schedule best. Allysha Lavino, a visionary writer, had just published her novel, *The Heretic,* in which she lays out the sacred geometry of the area. She studied with Henry Lincoln of *Holy Blood, Holy Grail* fame, who discovered this pattern in the valley and mountains that house so many sacred sites. But Allysha had canceled her 2021 tour as she was expecting a baby.

Even though the tour dates overlapped quite a bit with my teaching schedule, I decided to travel with Kathleen McGowan, who wrote the Magdalene Line trilogy. Her tour was organized by Body Mind Spirit Journeys, a company that used to run Stephen's tours, so this was a nice connection. I discovered when I signed up that the woman who used to help guide Kathleen's tours was recovering from serious surgery and a new guide would be working with her. Guess who? Veronique Flayol! Synchronicities were happening, which is always a positive sign.

Veronique Flayol & Kathleen McGowan in Montsegur
Photo by Theresa Crater

My most powerful experiences happened at the beginning and end of the tour. The first was in the town of Saint-Maximin-la-Sainte-Baume at the Basílica de Santa María Magdalena, where Mary Magdalene spent the last thirty years of her life. We visited her reliquary which houses her skull in the Basilica. Before the

French Revolution, the reliquary held more bones, but these were destroyed when many of the churches were ransacked during that period.

Standing in the square in front of the Basilica, Veronique explained the history of the place and how there had been a pagan temple here. Like so many places, the Magdalene taught in a sacred spot used by priestesses before her. Through research and aromatherapy training, Veronique recreated the oil the Magdalene used to anoint her beloved, Yeshua. She said, "I found the 'recipe' of the anointing oil in the Song of Songs and also in the Exodus." She let us put a few drops on our wrists, then instructed us to pass our wrists over our crown chakras. My inner vision opened up. The stone-cobbled square we were standing on turned into a green field with what I wanted to call a baptistry. I understood that people came to the Magdalene for her peace and for healing.

Some filming delayed our visit in the Basilica for about an hour, but once we were inside, Veronique took us close to the pulpit. Carvings depict the major events in the Magdalene's life. As Veronique spoke, I began to feel the Magdalene's presence. It became overwhelming, so I closed my eyes. The feelings intensified and she appeared before me, ripe with pregnancy. She pushed her belly up against me. Tears flowed and I tried to stay quiet so I wouldn't interrupt Veronique.

After she finished her talk, she invited us into the crypt a few at a time. Veronique explained her burial spot was in the old pagan temple and over the centuries, it had been buried. The cathedral is above it and we reached the crypt by going down ancient stone stairs. I felt enormous power and focus when I first glimpsed her skull in her gold reliquary; spiritual power and determination, but someone close to the front was snapping picture after picture, so it was difficult to keep my connection. I went back up the stairs and hoped to go back when things settled down. Tears kept leaking as I explored the cathedral. When I went back down into the crypt, I seemed to have acclimated to her energy. That first punch of power did not reoccur. I did not take a picture while I was in the crypt.

Although I've written about the bloodline, I didn't expect to have a strong personal connection with Mary Magdalene or any of the holy family, for that matter. But I was wrong. Mary Magdalene had reached out and grabbed me. Years before during the TM teacher training course I was finally able to attend, I had a visitation from Jesus and Mother Mary that was even more powerful and surprising. The year was 1975 and the place Vittel, France. During the group meditation before lunch, a golden light began to form above my head. With my inner vision, I looked up into the light. It fell on me, bathing me in unconditional love, healing everything it touched. I'd never before felt anything so pure, so divine.

Then a figure formed in the light. I saw a blue robe with white underneath and a white headdress. A woman. She held her hands out to her sides, palms forward, a posture you see in so many statues. The light flowed from her hands. I knew this was Mother Mary.

But I'm not Catholic, I thought.

This was waved away as irrelevant.

The figure rippled, like when we drop a pebble into a still pond, and the robe turned white. The feet had two red dots on them. As my gaze went up, I saw the red wounds in his hands, the gash in his side, and most surprising, the sacred heart shining in his chest. The white beneath the Mother's robe was replaced by a brown beard.

You see, we are one, he said.

And then they faded. I was left with a profound sense of peace and inner silence for a few days after.

Back in France in 2021, much farther to the south, our next stop was the grotto of Mary Magdalene, a wonderful cave up in the mountains near the city. The Magdalene spent a good deal of time in this wonderful cavern complete with freshwater pooling in the lower part. I never thought of the relics of saints or the places they spent time as being power spots, but France taught me otherwise.

I'd made the mistake of leaving Veronique's talk about the grotto before we started the hike because I'd had a hip replacement and had not exercised much during the pandemic, so I thought I would slow the group down. Going up the hill, I took a wrong turn that led to a much more difficult hike. I hadn't packed my hiking stick, opting for smaller luggage, but found a sturdy stick in the woods to help. I thought a few times of stopping and turning back, but finally made it, shaky with fatigue and drenched in sweat. Lesson learned.

In the grotto I sat off to the side, catching my breath and trying to tune into the space. After a bit, I explored, then returned to the front where Veronique was talking again. I couldn't really hear her since she spoke softly to avoid disturbing others, so I meditated. I had a brief vision of the top of the cave opening up to higher dimensions. I could sense that the Magdalene had communed with Yeshua there. She was indeed a spiritual adept. Like other times, this was just a picture in my head. No strong spiritual connection.

Grotto of Mary Magdalene
Photo by Theresa Crater

The natural cave is now filled with an altar and various statues of saints and angels. I wanted to sweep it all away, to just be in the natural cave. I thought of how Max had told me not to take his picture, not to get attached to his form. *It* (meaning Pure Consciousness) *will come to you in a different way next time*, he'd said. But now Stephen and I have a collection of crystal skulls. They are beautiful. They are good meditation tools. They increase the frequency of our house. But are they necessary? Were all these statues and the big altar in the Magdalene's grotto necessary, or a series of embroideries on the basic spiritual energy that existed there already?

I discovered a saint who shared my opinion of all this proliferation. After visiting the grotto, we drove to St. Marie de la Mer where we ate wonderful seafood and learned about Sarah and the three Marys. At a Roma camp we visited, Sarah had her own little caravan. I stuck my head in and she spoke to me. I realized that I was receiving many connections and sparks on this trip. Perhaps all that meditation over the years was paying off.

Sarah said that she came with Mary from Egypt. The French disagree with this, saying she was already there, that she was a queen of the Roma tribe who inhabited those shores at the time. Whichever is true, the story goes that Mary Magdalene, along with two other Marys, and perhaps Sarah, were put into a boat with no sail and no oars, and pushed into the Mediterranean from somewhere around Alexandria. The intent was to kill them, but their boat landed on the shores of what is now France. The group began sharing the teachings of Yeshua.

Our next trip was to the Église Sainte-Marthe de Tarascon. I didn't expect to connect in any way with Martha. I was wrong. Perhaps having no expectations is a part of being open to the energies that flood in. While waiting for the church to be opened for us, we went across the street to the castle. A statue of a strange beast sits to the side. Kathleen explained this was the *tarasque*, a river monster who terrorized the village until Martha made a deal with it. She told it the villagers would let it live if it stopped eating people, especially children. It agreed, but had one lapse. There is a statue inside the church of the *tarasque* with feet coming out of its mouth, looking a bit like "Oops, I forgot."

The church is built on Martha's original house. She was buried in that house which is, centuries later, now below the church. I felt a tug to go down. I descended the stairs, but the chapel in front of her sarcophagus was closed. I sat on the steps just outside, shut my eyes, and immediately found a deep well of peace. Deeper than I'd experienced for a long while. After a time, I opened my eyes and got back up. That's when she started talking to me.

She gestured to the cathedral and all its statues and the relic, all the stained glass and pews, as if to say, *Can you believe it? What's all the fuss? We shared a simple message and look what they've done with it.*

I smiled because this was how I'd reacted to the additions in the Magdalene's grotto.

Too much to dust, Martha summed up.

A world-famous psychic healer was one of the guests on the tour. I mentioned how peaceful the tomb site was and she came to check it out. On the way down the steps, she said that Martha was perplexed by the elaboration of the cathedral built over her simple house. I told her I'd had the very same impression.

On to Alet-les-Bains and the house of Nostradamus, where I got a little glimpse of him writing at a desk by the window of his room. We visited many of the Cathar sites in the surrounding towns and mountains. Based on my difficulty climbing up to the Magdalene's grotto, I decided not to climb Montségur. Others were deeply moved by the places we visited. Just like my experience in Egypt, people seem to be tuned to different sites.

Château d'Arques
Photo by Theresa Crater

I had relaxed into enjoying the beauty of France and learning about the history when toward the end of the tour we went to a small Cathar site sitting out by itself in the French countryside where I had perhaps the most profound experience of my life. This is what I wrote about the experience when I came home:

We are bedraggled pilgrims traveling in our bus through the beautiful countryside of southern France. We have come to find Mary Magdalene, to hear the stories of her, and discover our own truth about her. We have come to lay our burdens down, to heal, to find companionship on this stony path of life as we journey to find the perfection that is hiding in our hearts and has been with us always.

We climbed in 100-degree heat one day to the places where the Cathars lived in joy and were killed by fire or torture. We saw relics, visited cathedrals, and viewed the secret symbols. We dipped into the Mediterranean. We often ate two three-course meals of rich French food in one day and drank wine with each

*offering. We were greeted by the most generous hosts. We saw the
house of Nostradamus. This is just some of it.*

But I want to talk about the very last site on our itinerary.

*We have come to an ancient château named as the Container of
God. I'm about to find out why.*

*We climb the hill to this lone château sitting by itself in the
middle of beautiful fields, now golden in the late July sun. The
stones are a darker gold and resonate with a mellow peace. We
climb the hill, don our masks as we enter the outer office because
we are nearing the end of the pandemic and still must take some
precautions, and our intrepid leader buys our tickets.*

*I walk through the reception into the front yard of the
tower. Others have settled around a picnic table under the one
tree. I grab a plastic chair from a stack next to the wall and find a
spot under the blessed shade. The other pilgrims find places and as
they do, I feel a building peace. Something tugs at me to go over to
the side of the tower to a yard next to the stone wall that overlooks
the field and an abandoned farmhouse near a line of trees. But
Kathleen gathers the group and leads us in a meditation. We
breathe to settle into the place even more deeply and I stay in my
seat.*

*I begin to feel as if someone is over there in the field to the left
side, perhaps a tourist enjoying the ancient peace, and look up
from time to time to see if they will walk out. But no one comes.*

*Kathleen begins to tell her story about how this place revealed
so much on her journey to discover her life's work. I still feel that
mysterious presence, but now realize this is no ordinary tourist.
This presence is holy, sacred even, and I want to go discover who
or what it is. But Kathleen's story unwinds in a fascinating tale of
yearning for revelation and answers that come in miraculous
connections, and I want to hear this also. When she ends, I am
humbled and awed. Someone shares a beautiful poem that moves
me deeper into reverence, and as the group continues, I try to
sneak away quietly to find out what is pulling me.*

*As I walk into the field, the presence rises up in me. I lean
against the wall and close my eyes. Peace fills me, but it is more*

153

*than peace, it is a glorious, glowing consciousness, a radiant
presence. It is the divine awareness held here.*

*I open my eyes and look out into the mountains. Soft hills rise
and the valley cradles the sacred heart, pure love. Tears well and I
walk toward the stone wall. Should I let the tears come? Will I
disturb the group?*

*I go to the far corner and let my breath loose what is welling
up. At the wall I break down. I weep as the peace of the divine
consciousness fills me. I have found it once again and when I do
connect once more to the sacredness that has created all and filled
it with its glory, I weep. I weep because I release the pain of
separation. I am released from the crippling self-consciousness of
all my faults. How I say the wrong thing when I want to help. How
I judge when I know I should be compassionate. How I am harsh
when I want to be gracious. How I have failed in doing what I
came to do. Or perhaps failed isn't quite right, but I have not
brought the work to its perfect ripeness.*

*Perhaps we all weep during these experiences. We weep as the
wounds of our incarnation push forward to be comforted and
healed. We come in as perfect little sparks of that divine
wholeness, but our families have their wounds and these are
inflicted on our innocence. We go out into the world and are
disillusioned, disenchanted, hurt. And so we experience the fall
once again.*

*And once that is finished, once the wounds are healed, we
weep at the glorious perfection of it all—the golden grass, the
Queen Anne's lace blooming and expressing itself in flawless white
blossoms, little yellow flowers with their faces to the sun. We
realize that this divinity, this wholeness, is always there, flowing
like a river beneath it all. We weep in joy.*

*Then people are coming out from the group and I see the
one woman who expressed what I also felt. When Kathleen asked
for experiences, this woman tried to explain what she felt. "This
place is holy," she said, as she searched for words to express the
soft beating heart of God that lives here and has never been
tainted. I walk up to her, my face I'm sure red and ugly from*

*crying, and we embrace and she says, "I know. It is, isn't it?"
without me having to say anything except stumble with "It's just
so... It's just..." and I spread my arms wide to indicate the entirety
of it.*

*She understands. "Aucun mot ne saura exprimer ce que
tu ressens, " she says. There are no words.*

*The three sisters on the tour tell me later that they saw me
and held space for me as I went through my experience. I am
grateful.*

*If I could have sat and finished weeping, I know what
would have come next, because it always does. I would have been
filled with perfect peace. The peace that passeth all understanding.
I would have been balanced and gracious and all the things I
yearn to be always. I would have stayed in that divine union for as
long as my body and mind could have supported it. And then I
would have fallen again.*

Because this is the human condition.

*We carry with us our burdens, our imperfections. We get
irritated with others. We snipe. We criticize. We consume too much
plastic and pollute. We fall short.*

*But this is our job. To reconcile this physical incarnation,
this world, with the divine. And so we rise each day. We meditate
or pray or do the practice that brings us closest to balance, and we
go out and do our best.*

*After each encounter with the divine, we do not fall as far.
After each encounter, perhaps we snap a picture or buy a postcard
for our altar. Maybe we buy a necklace to touch so we remember
during the day the peace of that place. It is not the experience, but
a reminder.*

*May all who brought me to these experiences and places
be blessed. May their paths be strewn with rose petals. May the
scent of frankincense and myrrh waft across their faces. May their
way be smoothed. May their hearts be healed.*

*May we all succeed in raising the earth into perfection
again.*

WORKS CITED

Baigent, Michael, Richard Leigh & Henry Lincoln. *Holy Blood, Holy Grail: The Secret History of Christ & The Shocking Legacy of the Grail.* Dell, 2004.

Chaya, M.S. and H.R. Nagendra. "Long-term effect of yogic practices on diurnal metabolic rates of healthy subjects." *International Journal of Yoga.* 2008 Jan-Jun; 1(1): 27-32.

Childress, David Hatcher & Stephen S. Mehler. *The Crystal Skulls: Astonishing Portals to Man's Past.* Adventures Unlimited Press, 2008.

Close Encounters of the Fifth Kind: Contact Has Begun (2020). https://www.youtube.com/watch?v=CRK6IA--Swk

Crater, Theresa. *Beneath the Hallowed Hill.* Crystal Star Publishing, 2016.

---. *Under the Stone Paw.* Crystal Star Publishing, 2016.

Hafiz. "A Cushion for Your Head," *The Gift.* Translated by Daniel Ladinsky, Penguin, 1999, 183.

---. "Back Into Herself," *The Gift.* Translated by Daniel Ladinsky, Penguin, 1999, 131.

---. "I Imagine Now for Ages," *The Gift.* Translated by Daniel Ladinsky, Penguin, 1999, 209.

---. "Please," *The Gift*. Translated by Daniel Ladinsky, Penguin, 1999, 115.

---. "The Sun in Drag," *The Gift*. Translated by Daniel Ladinsky, Penguin, 1999, 252.

---. "What Happens to the Guest," *The Gift*. Translated by Daniel Ladinsky, Penguin, 1999, 178.

Hsin, Wu. *The Lost Writings of Wu Hsin*. Translated by Roy Melvyn, Summa Iru Publishing, 2011.

Knight, Gareth. *A Practical Guide to Qabalistic Symbolism*. Samuel Weiser, Inc., 1965.

Lavino, Allysha. *The Heretic*. White Cloud Press, 2020.

McGowan, Kathleen. Magdalene Line Trilogy. Atria Books, 2006-2010.

Mehler, Stephen. The Land of Osiris. Adventures Unlimited Press, 2001.

Ryder, Louise. *God in a Box*. Crystal Star Publishing, 2022.
Rumi. "Be Melting Snow," *The Essential Rumi*. Translated by Coleman Barks, Harper San Francisco, 1995, 13.

---. "Say I Am You," *The Essential Rumi*. Translated by Coleman Barks, Harper San Francisco, 1995, 275.

Wordsworth, William. "Lines Composed a Few Miles above Tintern Abbey, On Revisiting the Banks of the Wye during a Tour." July 13, 1798. www.poetryfoundation.org. Accessed 13 August 2022.

ACKNOWLEDGMENTS

I want to thank everyone who has helped me on my spiritual path. That is a long list, so I can't mention everyone by name. I especially want to thank Sarah Gabbay, Tom Kenyon, Mary Barbour, Jessie Mercay, and Ruth Adele. Thanks to Hakim Awyan, who taught me so much about Egypt. Many thanks to JoAnn Parks, Max's guardian who just keeps learning and growing, and Joe and Marylee Swanson for bringing Stephen to see Max and being such good folks. Also Kathleen McGowan, who taught me so much about Mary Magdalene and the bloodline.

Extra special thanks to Stephen Mehler. Ever since Max introduced us, we've had such amazing adventures together, and they're still unfolding.

Thank you, thank you Karen Stuth for your insightful editing and support in the publishing process. You're an amazing and talented person. I really appreciate Ann Mclean's translation help.

ABOUT THE AUTHOR

Born in North Carolina, Theresa Crater grew up during the civil rights movement, an experience that taught her anything is possible. She has studied Vedic philosophy and taught meditation since 1975, as well as worked with various forms of shamanism, Western metaphysics, and Reiki. A best-selling and award-winning author, Theresa brings ancient temples, lost civilizations, and secret societies back to life in her visionary fiction. She has nine novels out at present plus a handful of short stories. She lives in Boulder County with Egyptologist, writer, and tour guide Stephen Mehler, who co-founded Khemitology with indigenous wisdom keeper Ab'del Hakim Awyan. At present, Theresa and Stephen have one feline overlord. www.theresacraterbooks.com

ALSO BY THERESA CRATER

POWER PLACES SERIES

Under the Stone Paw
A forgotten family legacy. Six crystal keys. One shot at unlocking the secrets beneath the Sphinx.

Beneath the Hallowed Hill
Two legendary worlds. A disaster in the making. Can her psychic powers avert catastrophe?

Return of the Grail King
The long-awaited King Arthur returns to be reborn in the 21st century, but an old enemy from the past rises to stop him.

Into the City of Light
These legendary mystics want a peaceful life. But with the fate of humanity hanging in the balance, a new mission brings them too close to darkness.

Power Places Box Set
Books 1-3
Includes Under the Stone Paw, Beneath the Hallowed Hill, and Return of the Grail King.

POWER PLACES SHORT STORIES

"Frankincense and Myrrh"
Anne isn't letting Michael relax on Christmas Day. She's sent him on a treasure hunt inside the big Le Clair family house.

"Festival of Lights"

When Michael takes Anne and Arthur to celebrate the first night of Chanukah with his family, they're all in for a big surprise.

"A Star, A Star"

Morning Star, O cheering sight! 'Ere thou cam'st, how dark earth's night!

A brilliant, new star appears at Christmas in 2020. What does it foretell?

"Summer Solstice"

That child! Where did he disappear to now? Anne Le Clair talks Grandmother Elizabeth into celebrating summer solstice in Glastonbury. Little Arthur decides to pay a visit to another king. Will they find him before he gets lost in time?

STAND-ALONE

The Star Family

Whoever holds the key decides the future of humanity. when mysterious nighttime chanting leads Jane Frey to a secret chamber, she becomes entangled in a clandestine society with unsettling aims.

OTHER SHORT STORIES

"The Judgment of Osiris"

On the last day of the tour he leads, Owen accepts a gift from a rival tour guide Simon that contains a deadly poison. Will resurrection come for him as it did for his namesake Osiris or will his soul be consumed by Ammit?

"Bringing the Waters"

Nebit and Khai celebrate the Sacred Marriage. Each year the High Priestess of Hathor and High Priest of Horus unite sexually to bring on the flooding of the Nile. But this year, Nebit has another mission.

"White Moon"

When we call the Ancient Ones, sometimes they come. When Mayan Goddess Ixchel comes for her divine lover, lost in human form, her presence challenges the couples around her.

Theresa Crater's books and short stories are available on Amazon and at her website at www.theresacraterbooks.com. The short stories are available on major eBook sales sites.